WARRIORS BY BLOOD!

Born to Raze Hell

Volume One in
The Art of Spiritual War Series

Malcolm W. ("Chip") Hill. Jr.

AS HE IS, SO ARE WE IN THIS WORLD: WARRIORS BY BLOOD!

Table of Contents

FOREWORD

The Church of Jesus Christ is entering the most exciting stage of its history. As we enter the final days of this age, the command given to us by our Commander in Chief rings across the ages, "Go into all the world, and preach the gospel to all creation ... and these signs shall follow them that believe, in My name they will cast out demons ... they shall lay hands on the sick and they shall recover." I believe we are to fulfill that command in our generation.

This will entail a great confrontation with the powers of darkness. We must not shrink back in fear from this conflict, but with boldness, and under the anointing of the Holy Spirit, we must attack and overpower the "gates of hell."

I remember a fateful night in central Africa, where I was ministering the good news to a crowd of more than 200,000 natives. Most of them were in bondage to witchcraft. Thousands of sorcerers were in the crowd. As I ministered mass deliverance I saw literally thousands healed and delivered, with 25,000 decisions for Christ that evening. God had given me a rhema word, which became a mighty weapon against the powers of darkness that night. I declared to the crowd, "One drop of the blood of Jesus destroys the kingdom of Satan!" Evil forces trembled and fled at that declaration.

My friend, Chip Hill, has given us *Warriors by Blood!* This small volume, as well as the ones to follow in The Art of Spiritual War series, will help prepare the Church for its crucial end time role in human history. In the series, we will find many timeless principles that will enable Christians to successfully confront the powers of darkness in their generation, and bring forth the kingdom of Jesus. *Warriors by Blood*, will help to set the attitude of the Church for the awesome days that lie ahead.

I appreciate Chip's desire to serve the Body of Christ with this exciting new series. I highly recommend it to you. May the Lord Jesus Christ be exalted and His kingdom advanced through the study of these books.

Mahesh Chavda
Mahesh Chavda Ministries International

AUTHOR'S PREFACE

When the subject of spiritual warfare comes up, the minds of most believers settle on their own personal struggles in life. Whether they are facing a sickness, struggling with a financial crisis, or dealing with a besetting sin, the warfare is very real and disconcerting. Tribulations like these face all of us on this battlefield called earth. But too often the Christian's battle begins and ends right here, never branching out into the larger arena where the souls of others are concerned.

The warfare I primarily want to address in this book speaks to the arena of battle we call the harvest field. Indeed, the harvest field is a battlefield—a hotly contested piece of ground where each stalk of wheat is a human soul waiting to be gathered into the threshing barn of God's kingdom.

This harvest will only be gathered by an aggressive host of harvester/warriors who have conditioned themselves to endure the heat and sweat of the hour. Scripture shows that there are "appointed weeks of the harvest" (Jeremiah 5:24), and that a crop must be garnered at the right time or it will be lost. Beloved, that time is now! If we will pull ourselves from the shadows of our own self-focus, and thrust ourselves into the sweltering heat where earth's millions languish in despair, we will reap the final harvest, and rescue many from the misery of sin and spiritual death.

It seems that we are in the season the Bible calls

perilous times. Perhaps these times weigh more heavily upon us than time in any previous generation. As the threat of nuclear, chemical and biological warfare looms ominously on the horizon; as mounting fresh water crises, droughts and famines strengthen their grip on the nations; and as hopelessness and distress spread throughout the human race, the Church must gear up for what may be it's final onslaught against the forces of darkness.

Amidst the unfolding of this dramatic age, I want to offer the Church, *Warriors by Blood,* volume one in *The Art of Spiritual War* series. In it's pages, I hope to arouse the passions of all believers for the aggressive prayer and evangelism that are needed in this desperate hour, and yet are so often avoided by many in the Church.

Warriors by Blood is written to strengthen your resolve for reaching the world for Christ. It is designed to provide vital teaching concerning the reality and nature of the spiritual conflict in which we are presently embroiled.

In the series you will find many bite-sized war chapters, filled with quotations from many great people (past and present, spiritual and secular, military and civilian) who understood the principles that govern effective warfare, as well as the keys for survival in a harsh and unforgiving environment. Each volume will be steeped in Scriptures, addressing all aspects of spiritual warfare: prayer, evangelism, mercy ministries, disciple-making, church planting, deliverance and personal holiness. Scores of testimonies to encourage commitment to the work before us will also be given, as well as much prophetic insight concerning the critical times we are facing.

But again, my primary purpose for this volume is to call the Church to the front lines of aggressive evangelism. Without evangelism, the Church will not multiply and fill the earth. Without a continual stirring, spurring and provocation to reach the lost, most Christians will nestle down in their pews and stagnate.

At this writing I have been a believer for thirty years, and must sadly confess that I have never had anyone approach me, in private or in public, for the purpose of discussing the state of my eternal soul. I have not had so much as a tract handed to me while going about my daily affairs. I find this tragic. Are the Christians I encounter able to look at me and tell that I am already a believer, or is it that they just don't care to share their faith with anyone? I fear the latter reason prevails.

In the western Church many people pride themselves in how well they know the Bible, or how faithfully they keep a daily quiet time, but when it comes to evangelism, they do very little, if any thing at all. Knowing how to pray for finances, confess the promises, or worship with the latest praise CD, does little for the man down the street who is gripped in the snare of the Devil. That poor soul needs someone to release him in the power of Jesus' name!

As a whole, the Church is not very interested in evangelism, and if we believe that when the final harvest occurs, we will somehow benefit from it, we deceive ourselves. I have found that, more often than not, people reap as they have sown. If they have sparingly sown the seed of the gospel, then the crop they gather will be sparse at best.

Evangelism: Every Believer's Work

A fresh and vital mantle is falling today, begging the ordinary Christian to reach out, pick it up, and spread it upon humble shoulders. It is the end time mantle of evangelism—an anointing so powerful and compelling, that millions of people will be saved because of its presence on earth.

The mantle for reaching the world for Christ will not be placed entirely on the shoulders of multimedia evangelists. In addition to these devoted servants, the Lord wants to raise up hundreds of thousands of trench warriors—people like you and me—who will penetrate the highways and byways of worldly societies, persuading people to come into the sanctuaries of God.

Only the Lord knows exactly how much time remains before this age reaches its fitful climax, therefore, it behooves the Church—all who truly know and serve the Lord of armies—to enter the fray and pluck as many human brands from the burning as possible.

Beloved, we must act, and we must act now! If we are truly the generation "upon whom the ends of the ages have come" (1 Corinthians 10:11), then we must get busy, because our season of harvest may soon end. Until then, the battle is on for the souls of men! The world is up for grabs!

1
An Army With Banners

Too often the teaching of spiritual warfare is faddish and superficial, only producing weekend warriors instead of lifetime combatants. At all times, however, the teaching is essential. While we should never be too fascinated by our fight against the kingdom of darkness, neither should we be unmindful or apathetic. The Devil is never more successful than when accosting a church that is ignorant of his devices and oblivious to its authority in Christ. Conversely, he is never more a failure than when facing a church that knows well the principles of warfare, as well as it's authority to wage it.

This book comes out of an innate desire to help prepare a people for the tumultuous days we are fast entering. I make no claim to great scholarship concerning this vital subject, but as a fellow soldier who has seen a fair share of conflict through the years, I want to stir you to bold action for the King and His kingdom. Facing the reality and the brutality of spiritual warfare requires courage, and courage requires bold action.

As I write these words, a song from the great Gettysburg soundtrack rises from my laptop. Fittingly, the song is named: "Over the Fence." I pray that as you read this volume, you will be encouraged to leave the comfort of familiar surroundings and force yourself "over the fence," so that you might fearlessly assault the kingdom of darkness and bring the kingdom of God in your generation.

The Military Image

The Bible uses many metaphors to describe God's people on earth. They are seen as a legislative body, an assembly, a family, a priesthood, pilgrims and sojourners, a temple, a building, a field, a kingdom, and as a bride espoused to Christ. But that's not all. When describing the Church as that which is betrothed to Jesus, the Scripture also sets forth the image of an awesome army with banners (Song 6:4, 10). As far back as the wilderness wanderings, God used banners as a rallying point for His people.

The people of Israel must camp around the Tent of Meeting. But they must not camp too close to it. All of them must camp under their flags and under the banners of their families. The companies of the camp of Judah must be on the east side. They must set up camp toward the sunrise. They must camp under their flag.

Numbers 2:2-3, NIRV

According to Dr. Eugene H. Merrill, (The Bible Knowledge Commentary), banners (' t t, v.2) or flags identified the individual families, and a standard (*de al*, vv. 2-3) identified each three-tribe division. These standards made the mighty army seem more beautiful to its friends and more formidable to its enemies. When time came for the armies of Israel to march, "the companies of Judah went first. They went out under their flag" (Numbers 10:14). The other companies followed in like manner, marching forth beneath their respective standards. Imagine the trepidation felt by sentries in ancient Canaanite and Philistine cities when, peering from watchtowers on their walls, they beheld unfurled war banners waving above the dust covered divisions of Israel's massive army. The fear that struck them must have been paralyzing.

But what about God's marching host in our dispensation? With Christ's love being the banner over the Church today (Song 2:4), and Jesus Himself being the rallying Banner for the nations (Isaiah 11:12), the trepidation felt by the Devil and his wicked hordes must be immense. Certainly they cringe at the sight of millions of Christians blanketing the globe with the glorious gospel. They know their time is short, and must therefore be horrified!

For centuries banners have been used to identify and rally troops for battle. Banners should encourage confidence in the warriors who march beneath them. Prophetically voicing their faith, David's host declared a confidence that God would answer their king's prayer for victory. They said, "We will sing for joy over your (David's) victory, and in the name of our God we will set up our banners!" (Psalm 20:5).

Relating this verse to our day and time, we replace king David with King Jesus, and prophetically declare His victory over every enemy, raising our banners as symbols of our confidence in Him. Indeed, the Church triumphant is a host deployed beneath the blood-stained banner of God's love, and we who march with the "Commander of the army of the Lord" (Joshua 5:14), are a terrible sight for demon powers to behold! Truly, the One given as "a leader and commander for the people," has raised a banner over those who fear [Him], that it may be displayed because of the truth! (See Song 2:4; Isaiah 55:4. Psalm 60:4.)

Beloved, the next time you see someone waving a banner in the praise portion of a worship service, see it through the eyes of the enemies of God. Better yet, look at it from God's perspective; it is precious in His sight.

15

A Universal Battle

The Church's battle is global in proportions, limited not only to the visible realm, but extending also into the invisible realm, impacting spiritual "thrones, dominions, principalities and powers." (See Colossians 1:16; Ephesians 3:10; 6:12). Our authority carries weight in every realm of existence, because Jesus' name carries weight in every realm, and we have the duty to use His name in prayer and spiritual warfare. That is why the Lord assured us, saying, "whatever you bind on earth will be bound in heaven, and whatever you loose on earth will be loosed in heaven" (Matthew 16:19). The Greek word, *ourano,* translated "heaven" in this verse, refers to the sky or air above us.[1] It can mean Heaven, the place where God lives, or it can mean the atmosphere about his planet—the location where Satan's throne is situated. As "the prince of the power of the air" (Ephesians 2:2), Satan is identified as a wily adversary, situated at the head of spiritual hosts of wickedness in heavenly places (Ephesians 6:12). Nevertheless, in Jesus' preeminent name, we have authority to contend with him and his warriors, compelling them to submit to God's agendas. The Church on earth is an occupying army, adorned in spiritual regalia and equipped with a supply of weapons that are irresistible when wielded in the love of God.[2]

Fundamental Distinctions

The primary differences between God's spiritual army and the natural armies of men are found in both their purposes and methods. Natural armies either fight *unjust* wars for the gluttonous expansion of their own interests, or they fight *just* wars for the safety of their own citizens, or the emancipation of oppressed people within other nations.

As the pillar and ground of the truth, the Christian army

16

is to engage in an honorable spiritual battle, fulfilling the Great Commission and seeking to save those lost in sin and it's horrible consequences (Luke 19:10). Jesus summed up the overall mission of the Church when He commissioned Paul, saying, "I am sending you to open their eyes, and to turn them from darkness to light, and from the power of Satan unto God, that they may receive forgiveness of sins, and inheritance among them which are sanctified by faith that is in me" (Acts 26:18, KJV). If we are righteous warriors, then this is our primary assignment in life. Let us never lose sight of it.

Satanic Strongholds

The Lord's army is also distinctive because of the weapons it takes up—weapons that are not physical, but spiritual in their origin and application. The Bible promises that when used properly, these weapons will pull down the blinding, binding strongholds erected in the minds of men. (See 2 Corinthians 10:4).

In his classic, *The Three Battlegrounds,* Francis Frangipane expounds on our battle against these strongholds:

> *There are satanic strongholds over countries and communities; there are strongholds that influence churches and individuals. Wherever a stronghold exists, it is a demonically-induced pattern of thinking. Specifically, it is a "house made of thoughts" which has become a dwelling place for satanic activity.[3]*

Too often, when visualizing the battle against

strongholds, Christians see castle-like fortresses sitting somewhere in the atmosphere above where they are. They then attempt to overwhelm and pull them down by shouting loud demands, in Jesus' name. More often than not, this is a misguided application of spiritual power. The strongholds we are to assail are not located in the spiritual atmosphere in the sky above us, so much as they are found in the natural and carnal minds of men. While it is true that in most cases a principality or ruling spirit in heavenly regions calls the shots for demonically-induced strongholds of the mind, the strongholds themselves are built in the thought-patterns and belief systems of men. Paul pinpointed these fortresses when he told us to bring "every thought into captivity to the obedience of Christ" (2 Corinthians 10:5). As Frangipane said, the strongholds are located in the minds, thought patterns, and faulty beliefs of men. No amount of shouting will overwhelm these bastions of mental bondage. Only calculated prayer, worship, and a pinpointed application of God's Word will overcome such strongholds.
(and fasting)

Toppling Strongholds

It should be understood that the first strongholds to be conquered by Christians are those found within themselves. These fortresses are either mental or spiritual in nature. Untamed attitudes and motives that work crosswise to God's will are rooted in the spirits of men—often going deeper than the carnal mind can readily grasp. Spiritual poisons like resentment, rage, envy, jealousy and pride, are spiritual in nature—the sour products of spiritual strongholds. A person's craving for recognition and popularity might be rooted in the spiritual stronghold of rejection. These strongholds and the demons that exploit them are the engines that drive a person to think and act the way that they do.

Strongholds such as confusion, ignorance, deception, and the psychological weaknesses of anxiety, fear and depression, are generally rooted in mental strongholds.

In addition to these negative symptoms, physical infirmities are often rooted in these spiritual or mental strongholds. For example: arthritis (joint inflammation) may be the product of an inflamed attitude of heart that refuses to forgive. The little old lady with gnarled hands and fingers just might have a gnarly root of bitterness in her heart that goes back forty years—to when someone offended her and got away with it. If the inflamed spirit does not manifest in a physical infirmity, it may manifest in a mental disorder. Indeed, many patients who are bad enough to be institutionalized are there because they will not forgive someone from their past. The human mind and body were not made to carry negative emotions for long periods of time. When forced to do so, they become sick and infirm. A negative stronghold of mind and/or spirit functions like a fortified castle on a hill; reigning over an entire region, making everyone sick, broke and miserable.

A deepening prayer life and ample time in the Word of God will weaken and eliminate every stronghold if we will only get down to business with God. As we grow in biblical knowledge and experience, daily conforming to the image and nature of Christ, a transformation of mammoth proportions will occur, compelling each and every demonic stronghold to crumble. I once heard Derek Prince say that we can make things so nice inside for Jesus that demons will want to pack up their baggage and leave. Strongholds crumble as we grow in the knowledge of who we are in Christ, and begin to order our lives by that wonderful knowledge.

Even so, there are those who argue that gaining personal

freedom is impossible for some, and that asking them to give themselves to vital time in the Word and prayer is an unreasonable request. They argue that some folks are just too far down in the dumps to be able to worship their way to victory. Unless they have severe brain damage, I disagree; particularly when there are examples to study like that of the Gadarene demoniac. Nothing an indwelling legion of demons did could stop this man from falling down before the Lamb of God in worship, and it was in worship that he found deliverance (See Mark 5:1-6.) The Lord will never allow someone's ability to worship Jesus to be taken away. Each of us has the will to pursue Him for whatever we need.

Laying Up a Siege

In some warfare situations, it becomes necessary for an attacking army to lay siege to the fortified position of an opposing force. When doing so the goal is to hem in and surround the enemy, cutting off his supply lines, and forcing his surrender.

When one lays siege to a demonic stronghold, he must use the same basic laws of the siege, and surround the fortress with all that he has at his disposal. Daily he must bombard it with the truth that liberates, as well as unyieldingly cut off the supply lines that seek to feed it.

For example: If one has a stronghold of sexual lust that needs to be overthrown, he should avoid what has fed the lust through the years. If he fails to do this, he will fight a losing battle. It may be that television, magazines, or the internet, with their copious images of beautiful men and women, are major supply lines into the stronghold in his life. The power God gives him to conquer lust will be neutralized by the images he sees if he keeps those images coming.

20

Whether we are confronting lust, a fortress of depression and fear, or some other formidable stronghold, the principle works the same. Lay up a siege with truth, and cut off the supply lines to the evil stronghold!

A verse in Proverbs applies here. It says, "Where no wood is, there the fire goes out" (26:20). This principle is extremely simple: Stop giving the fire what it needs to burn, and before long it will die! No stronghold will remain if placed under siege.

But how is the serious spiritual warrior, already free himself, to effectively rid the minds of others from these life-sapping fortresses?

First, by tough, pinpointed prayer for those held captive by the strongholds. Through consistent, clear-cut prayer to the Father, we can set up and lay a military siege on the minds of anyone we want to see liberated from demonic deception. We do not seek to take over or control the minds of the individuals, but we do seek to liberate them from unscriptural influences so that they might hear and understand the truth as it comes to them.

Second, we bind the demonic forces that feed the strongholds, cutting off what supply lines we can, in Jesus' name! We must do this daily or the supply lines to the strongholds will remain unchallenged, and the victimization of the individual(s) will be sustained. The spiritual authority we have as Christians is much more far-reaching than many of us believe. We must pray and war by faith, however, if we will see the results we desire.

One of my sons came under the influence of a worldly and sensual girl when he was in high school. Not only did the girl go after him, but her mother did as well. She seemed determined to secure our son for her daughter.

When we realized what was happening, Darlene and I went immediately to prayer. A hill I call Jawbone Heights rises just to the southeast of our home. It was on Jawbone Heights in Israel that Samson slew a thousand Philistines with the jawbone of an ass, and it is on Jawbone Heights in Mill Gap, Virginia, where I have eliminated thousands of demons in spiritual combat.

Out on this hill, Darlene and I began to address the demons of seduction and witchcraft that were working within the girl to captivate our son. We demanded that they cease and desist in their strategy to deceive and entice him. We also bound the spirits that were blinding him to the mortal danger. Women like these have the power to derail a man's destiny in God, and we were not going to allow that to happen! With determination, we employed the weapons of praise, intense fervent prayer, and pinpointed spiritual decrees. We prayed for God to drive a wedge between these women and our son, and were determined to war until he was free from their influence. After an hour or so, the Lord blessed us with an inner note of victory—a deep sense that we had gained our objective. Within the week victory was manifested as the mother and daughter turned their affection on someone else. In warfare we had cut off both suppliers and supply lines, and hadn't said a word to anyone but God and the demons involved.

The third thing we must do to free another person from the power of a stronghold is deliver the Word of God to their minds, replacing deception with the truth. Most people who reject biblical truth only do so because of the lies Satan has lodged in their minds. These strongholds are better established than the small amounts of truth they've heard, and so we must beef-up our efforts at getting more truth to them. This is why evangelism and disciple-making are so very important, and must not be left up to a few faithful servants. God needs an army to carry out this part of the warfare. Paul asks, "And how shall they believe in Him of whom they have not heard? And how shall they hear without a preacher?" (Romans 10:14). Every Christian is called to preach the gospel—to replace deception and ignorance with truth. Every Christian is called to help disciple those from the nations who turn to Christ. We may rip a demon from a person's mind and cause him to turn from the lie he once held as true, but unless we educate him with the Word of God, he is doomed to fall back into error and captivity. Indeed, it is not enough to sweep and garnish the house from which we've driven a demon or pulled down a stronghold, but we must also fill the house with the abundance of God's Life and Word so there will be lasting victory. (See Luke 11:24-26.)

ENDNOTES

1. Robert Young, *Young's Analytical Concordance to the Bible,* Hendrickson Publishers, Peabody, MA., p. 471.
2. The weapons God has given the Church are spiritual and supernatural. They are the Name of Jesus, the Word of God, the blood of Jesus, the word of our testimony, the gifts of the Holy Spirit, the power of decree, and spiritual praise and worship. Later in this series we will examine these weapons in detail.
3. Francis Frangipane, *The Three Battlegrounds,* Advancing Church Publications, Marion, Iowa, 1989, P. 20.

2
A People Poised for Battle

The Lord's army is poised to execute lightning-fast rescue operations deep into enemy held territory. Prisoners-of-war, lost and blinded to truth, are held there in dismal captivity, awaiting a life-giving word. They are the weak, sick and hopeless among us, the mass of men and women who Thoreau said, "lead lives of quiet desperation."

Perhaps the checkout lady down at the local market is one of these prisoners. Recently, arthritic flare-ups have threatened to force her from the job she cannot afford to abandon. What can you do to keep that from happening?

Perhaps one of these desperate prisoners is the widower whose path you frequently cross when you go into town. This poor soul may see his life as worthless since the passing of his wife, but a gentle hand on the shoulder and loving words are all he needs to give him hope for better days to come. My daughter, Ashton, set her heart on such a man not long ago, making it her aim to touch his life with Jesus' love whenever she saw him in a local restaurant. On several occasions she asked him to give his heart to Christ. He hemmed and hawed at her suggestion, but never blatantly rejected it. Only eternity will tell the impact she made in the waning years of his lonely life. When news came of his death, we embraced the hope that her gentle witness had made a difference before it was too late. Perhaps on the lonesome, frightening bed of death, this solitary soul made his peace with God. Perhaps in the final hours of his life, he heard again the gentle nudging of a little girl who loved enough to tell him about Jesus.

Dare to do Something!

A lady in our church is a wonderful example of what it is to be a revival warrior on a local level. Whenever she learns of someone in our community who is beset with sickness and/or despair, she contacts them, offering what will be a steady stream of blessing in the form of Bible teaching tapes, books, lists of healing Scriptures, phone calls, and cards of encouragement. She even contacts beleaguered souls in other regions when they come to her attention. A lady with cancer in a distant city recently shared how this gal has been nothing but a source of encouragement during her prolonged bout with the malignant disease.

This revival-warrior may not be a minister of world renown, but she is a vessel of pure gold to the people who meet her at their time of great need. We regularly learn of how people were healed, or had financial breakthroughs, or were saved as a result of her compassion.

Too often, Christians feel that unless they conduct great crusades like well-known evangelists and teachers, then they are not worth very much to the Lord. But this is not true. Statistics reveal that the Church worldwide is growing faster through compassionate one-on-one ministries than by all the gospel crusades put together! I thank God for the powerful platform preachers and their massive meetings, but I thank Him more for the little heroes who are winning the battle in the streets, touching every day people in every day ways.

Wherever one cares to look, there are spiritual hostages—precious souls trapped and tortured by a taskmaster whose appetite for the suffering of others is gargantuan. Their numbers boggle our minds, men and women crying within for someone to lift their burdens, for someone to lead them from the madhouse of despair.

Many in this troubled world have yet to hear the gospel for the first time. Even in the West there are those who have not heard that Jesus suffered the penalty for mankind's sin. In Charlotte, North Carolina, for example, I met a young man in the city's slums who had never heard the story of redemption. Although he wore a little cross around his neck, he had no idea what it represented. As I spoke to him of eternal truth, he fondled the precious emblem with tender appreciation, staring wide-eyed as the light dawned in his heart. And while sharing with him, I perceived that he was only one of thousands in his city who knew Jesus only as a long-gone historical or mythological oddball, and not as the ascended Son of God, Messiah.

Beloved, we must permeate society and announce that Jesus is alive, that He loves all men, and will never be more willing to save them than He is right now. If we fail in this task, we may delay the hour of awakening God longs to bring to our respective region. Preaching the gospel is every believer's calling—his life's blood! When we fail to exercise ourselves in this worthy vocation, spiritual passion cools and the joy of faith begins to wane. Examine yourself, beloved; when was the last time you impacted someone for Christ? If it was long ago, you must admit that something precious has seeped from your life. Never are we more vigorous than when touching and reaching other lives for God.

No Distinction

Let there be no distinction between clergy and laity

where this vital work is concerned. Every believer is called to liberate those locked in the clammy clutches of spiritual death. Truly, the greatest soul-winners of any generation should be those not even serving in pastoral leadership. They should be every day people, experiencing lives of joy and enthusiasm while working or playing among the downtrodden masses. A passion for the lost should carry these soul winners from day to day. Like avid fishermen, they should long to wet their lines in the vast ocean of humanity that surrounds them, and bring in a massive catch. After presenting their catch to their pastors for oversight, they should again wade into society's violent riptides, and pluck more souls from the depths of bondage. This cycle should constantly repeat itself until the fullness of the Gentiles has come in. Indeed, each believer's life should be one massive and on-going fishing trip.

Not only should we view soul winning as fishing, but we should also see it as the reaping of a harvest. The souls of those around us are like ripe wheat standing in a field, ready to be cut down and gathered into the barn of God's kingdom. We should not only pray for the Lord to send laborers into this vast harvest field, but we should also embrace our own responsibility to swing the sickle of the Lord. May we stop fantasizing about winning the lost someday and begin doing it today!

I composed the following poem to express my heart concerning this matter:

Grasp the Sickle

Grueling hours man is facing,
Time is short, extend a hand;
Grasp the sickle's well-worn handle,
Rally 'round the Son of Man.

Desperate souls in fields awaiting,
Fraught with fear - no time to spare!
When we ask them, some will gladly
Meet the loving Savior there.

Forlorn souls we will encounter
As we journey near and far;
Today they rest in deepest slumber,
Locked in living death they are.

If we fail to stir our passions
For this generation dear,
We will know humiliation,
When we see the Savior's tear.

We'll recall their names and faces,
Terror striking each dead heart,
Recognize our friends and neighbors,
At yon awful Judgment Bar.

Now's the time to grasp the sickle,
Swing with passion, swing with fear;
Reap the souls of dying humans,
Bless His heart, our Savior dear.

— M. H.

Why Must They Wait To Hear?

I was twenty-one before I heard my first gospel message, and I grew up in "Christian" America! At church, I was raised on spiritual ice cream and cookies, but not on Jesus. By the time I reached adolescence I was accustomed to the stale, dried out crumbs of liturgical religion, and knew nothing of my need for a life-changing encounter with Jesus. Regrettably, that's how it was for most in my generation,

29

and like so many others during that time, I turned to the illicit and fleeting pleasures of sin.

Spiritual ignorance is not confined to one age group, nor is the terrible suffering it produces in the lives of those plagued with it. By the time I was twenty years old an overwhelming number of problems were ruining my life. Besides an ever-increasing addiction to beer and bourbon, I found myself utterly enslaved to pornography. Not only that, but my heart was filled with bitterness and rage toward many who had wronged me in life. Horrible nightmares frequently spoiled my sleep, leaving me with intense feelings of despair. A severe case of arthritis started crippling my young body, and the notion that I would ever enjoy a sufficient supply of finances was quickly becoming an illusion. Many in my generation were experiencing similar levels of desolation.

Late in the 1960's, something wonderful began to happen among the youth in America: The Jesus Movement erupted among the hippies and baby-boomers, and many were plucked as brands from the burning. Having already given themselves to lifestyles that defied the blundering political establishment of the day, they were ready to bypass the bumbling religious establishment as well. Rather than yield their revolutionary spirit to those who would water down or kill it, they began to cry out to God for His guidance into new frontiers. As a result, thousands of vibrant works began worldwide; many remain strong till this day! If cold orthodoxy had seized these young zealots, it would have made them twofold the sons of hell as anyone Jesus encountered in Jerusalem. (See Matthew 23:15.) But thank God, that did not happen but in a few cases! This radical new generation of misfits pressed forward in the face of all odds, blazed new trails, and established awesome strongholds for God throughout society! But their paths were fraught with danger. Much pride and stubbornness had to be pressed out of these warriors. The restlessness and resistance to authority that identified them in the 60's and 70's had to be rooted out if they would become the leaders God wanted for the 80's, 90's, and beyond. Indeed, the closing decades of the twentieth century saw tens of thousands of these men and women go through torturous seasons of pruning and adjustment. Though rebellion toward cold, lifeless orthodoxy, spared them one set of problems, it also created many others. (Resistance to death-dealing religion is no excuse for cocky independence.) Many who were saved and set into ministry during or just after the hippie era, fell by the wayside, unwilling to endure the Lord's chastening hand. Others abandoned faith and ministry because they were unable to tolerate the warfare Satan brought against them. However, the many who endured turned out to be the highly trained veterans who today are leading the troops into the epic battles of the last days. God is now looking for men and women with the guts to follow them! He is presently looking for men and women with the burning passion to shout truth from the housetops!

Your troops will be willing to fight for you on the day of battle.

Psalm 110:3a, NIRV

The Lord is now recruiting willing warriors, men and women who refuse to settle down behind the dull, cozy walls of conventional Christianity. He yearns for revolutionary soul-winners who will charge into earth's hottest places of battle, and reap a giant end time harvest! Will you be included in their number? Will you venture forth onto the highways and byways, and into the homes

31

and businesses where lost humanity is gathered in eternal despair? It will not always be easy to persuade men to believe, but still we must offer them the only true hope they will ever have.

Let me close this chapter with a testimony from the memoirs of William Carvosso, a class leader for early Methodism who exhibited a bulldog tenacity when going after souls.

February 20, 1825 — *A few days ago I went to visit a sick man. I had been with him before, and found him very dark and ignorant. I had asked him if he ever prayed; and he told me that he did. I inquired what he prayed for, and he replied, "That God would take me to Heaven." "And what would you do in Heaven in your sins?" I asked. "Heaven is no place for an unregenerate soul. God's word is gone forth, 'Without holiness no man shall see the Lord;' and, therefore," I said, "except you repent you must perish."*

I now found him much distressed in mind; he said he had not rested since my conversation with him. When I beheld him in this state on the brink of eternity, it is impossible to describe the love and pity I felt for him. He knew but little, having never been able to read the word of God. I gave him all the help I could; and though a despairing gloom pervaded his mind, a ray of hope would occasionally animate his feelings. In speaking to him of the consolations of Divine mercy, I was wonderfully assisted; but in the course of a few hours he died. The strong compassion I felt for him, connected with those marks of penitence which he manifested, forbid me to entertain the thought that he is eternally lost; but this matter must be left to the decision of the great day.

Beloved, our job is to plead with men to give their lives to Jesus. Only the Christian with an eye on eternity can grasp the importance of this crucial business. We are not selling earthly commodities here; we are offering men eternal life. But they must repent, and must be told so! They must embrace the Master, and must be told so! They must embark on lives of holiness, and must be told so! They must reckon themselves as dead to the world, and must be told so! For when Christ calls a man to follow Him, He bids him come and die! *Amen*

3
Warriors By Blood!

The reasons for enlisting in the natural army are varied. Some men join because they need a job, and feel that the army pays well enough. Perhaps they like the idea that the army will pay for their college education when they get out. Others enlist because their country is under attack by hostile forces, and they feel like joining to defend their country is the right thing to do. Still other men join the army because they get drafted, and they have no choice but to sign up. During some wars in the past, there were men who joined the army because they were ashamed not to. Not to fight for your country when many of the boys you grew up with were fighting would bring a certain amount of disgrace on you and your family.

However, their is another type of individual who goes to war for an entirely different reason. This is the guy who is simply a warrior by blood. A proclivity for war is part of his DNA! He lives to fight the bad guys and free the good guys!

In the movie, *Rambo III,* Special Forces Colonel Troutman attempts to draw a former protégé, John Rambo, out of seclusion and into a covert mission gearing up in the Middle East. When the colonel realizes that Rambo has no inclination to accompany him in the operation, he asks the skilled warrior, "Johnny, when are you going to come full circle, and accept who you are?" Rambo immediately questions, "Sir, who am I?" Troutman accurately replies, "You're a pure fighting machine, Johnny, and you'll never be satisfied until you accept who you really are!"

When it comes to eternal matters where the souls of men are concerned, Christians are spiritual fighting machines. Whether we know it or not, the stuff that makes us powerful prayer warriors and effective soul winners is in our blood. It is part of our spiritual DNA.

Jesus Himself is the consummate spiritual warrior. He is literally endued with an unction for war; it is a part of who He is. "The Lord is a man of war; the Lord is His name" (Exodus 15:3). We cannot deny the fact that Jesus is "commander of the army of the Lord" (Joshua 5:14), and when He returns in glory, He is coming on the white horse of victory as militant King of kings, and Lord of lords! (Revelation 19:11-16).

But what about you and me? We know that Jesus is a warrior, but it doesn't come quite so naturally to many of us. Like one sister recently told me: "I'm just not a warrior. I feel like this church expects everyone to be warriors, and I can't do it." Is it that she *can't* be a warrior, or that she *won't* be one? Beloved, I don't see where we have a choice. Being on this earth necessitates that we fight or become casualties! If not for anyone else, we must learn to stand and fight the Devil for ourselves, or he will dominate us.

We say that Jesus' blood has washed us, yet we have never seen or felt it; it is a spiritual reality that impacts our lives in every way. We say that Jesus' blood has sanctified, redeemed, and justified us, but again, we have never seen or felt it; it is a spiritual reality that impacts our lives in every way. Doesn't it stand to reason then, that if Jesus' blood impacts us in so many remarkable ways, that its supernatural flow through our spiritual veins will transform us into heavenly style warriors as well—making us warriors by blood? Indeed it does; we just need to get in touch with the reality of it. It is not that we crave or go about looking for opportunities to fight, but if ever times arise when evil must be confronted and crushed, we are anointed to do it in Jesus' name.

Commenting on our relationship with Jesus, John declared: "...as He is, so are we *in this world*" (1 John 4:17). Take a moment to ponder what he is saying in this verse.

Is Jesus a lover? Yes! And so are we, because "the love of God has been poured out in our hearts by the Holy Spirit who was given to us" (Romans 5:5). The Holy Spirit is the agent by which God's love applies in and through our lives.

Is Jesus a fruit-bearing Vine? Yes! And so are we, because the Holy Spirit produces these fruits on the branches of the true Vine, whose branches we are. (See John 15:4-5; Galatians 5:22-23).

Is Jesus a mighty warrior, armed against the works of darkness? Yes, and so are we, because *as He is, so are we in this world!* Indwelt by the Holy Spirit, the warfare mantle of Jesus falls to you and me! Throughout the Scriptures, we see the Spirit of God stirring up His people against evil. The Holy Spirit incited Saul to demolish the army of Nahash the Amonite for threatening the children of Jabesh Gilead. The Holy Spirit stirred Deborah to assemble an army against Jabin, evil king of Canaan. The Holy Spirit came mightily upon Samson, inciting him to tear apart a fierce lion that confronted him, as well bludgeon one thousand Philistines with the jawbone of an ass. And what about the New Testament? Are there any examples of such stirrings found there? Indeed there are: The Holy Spirit moved Paul to confront demonic lies in the city of Athens with the truth that would set men free. In the city of Philippi, the Holy Spirit stirred him to action against a spirit of divination that worked in a slave girl to discredit his ministry. The Holy Spirit, if allowed to stir God's people, will always incite them to righteous warfare with evil! As we march through this world as pilgrim soldiers, we are called and equipped to "wage the good warfare" (1 Timothy 1:18); "fight the good fight of faith" (1 Timothy 6:12); "pull down strongholds, cast down arguments, and bring unscriptural thoughts into captivity" (2 Corinthians 10:4-5); "wrestle principalities and powers" (Ephesians 6:12); "resist the devil" (James 4:7), and "contend earnestly for the faith which was once for all delivered to the saints" (Jude 3). There is no way we can do this without becoming partakers of the divine nature (2 Peter 1:4). As new creations and ambassadors for Christ, we are called to grapple with evil spirits in the unseen realm. Old Testament warriors were called to contend with flesh and blood enemies, but New Testament warriors are commissioned to advance against the spiritual forces of darkness that keep men in spiritual, mental and physical bondage. As warriors by blood, we live to set men free!

Warrior By Blood

Standing on the firing line,
A soldier poised for war,
As angry principalities
Confront him with a roar.
Determined to ignore their ruse,
He stands secure in grace.
This host of one then moves ahead,
Determined in his pace.

Arrayed in holy armor,
Endued with Heaven's power,
This champion of desperate times
Has souls to save this hour.
As sounds of battle rip the sky,
This humble one appeals
To Heaven's God with open heart,
"Make me a man of steel!"

"It's in your blood!" the Lord replies,
"War is your vital breath!
Now is the time, look deep inside,
You'll find it in your breast!
Propensity, proclivity,
You'll see it comes quite naturally.
You'll wage this war in gallant style,
Against all principality!"

In noble form, with charity,
Traversing native land,
This warrior snatches dying men
From fire souls like brand.
When enemies of God attempt
To shut his mission down,
He yet holds forth in Spirit power
And grinds them in the ground.

With Word of God and praising lips
This valiant man appears,
Upon the scene of mortal men,
Within specific years;
To give his life for Heaven's cause,
He's seeking those to save;
Yes, those allotted to his charge,
Despite the Devil's rage.

Though hearts of men are often cold,
Locked in a frozen sway,
This champion of God looks up,
Prays down a melting ray.
In agony and heart despair,
The demons stare in awe,
As angels join with Holy Ghost,
Producing Heaven's thaw.

Revival fire then fills the land,
Awakening breaks forth;
God's army strong is multiplied
To hold redemption's torch.
And when the faithful warrior dies,
In Heaven he will see,
The blood-bought souls that he has won
For all eternity.

— M. H.

The Desperate Ground of Calvary

A lonely windswept hill outside the walls of ancient Jerusalem was once the scene of earth's most horrific battle. In its long history, the ground had been soaked with the blood of many warriors, but nothing compared with the brutality that would occur as the Son of God was crucified for the sins of mankind. His was not only a physical bludgeoning, but a spiritual one as well; an experience worse than a million deaths. You see, Jesus was cut off from His Heavenly Father for the first time in His eternal existence. It was a hideous battle! Amidst the agonizing dark moments of this heroic conflict, God's Son cried in a most abandoned and dejected tone: "My God, my God, why have You forsaken me?" Imagine that! God was crucifying Himself

40

on the cross. If you and I could somehow hear the pain that filled that solitary voice, we would never again return to sin in any form. O, how He must have loved us! Now we have a moral obligation to live in holiness.

Entering battle on the desperate ground of Golgotha, Jesus set in motion a legal transaction that would purchase salvation for men everywhere and for all time. Not only that, but He also secured a bright future for this cursed planet. Scripture promises that at the revealing of the sons of God, "the creation itself will be delivered from the bondage of corruption into the glorious liberty of the children of God" (Romans 8:21). The victory gained at Calvary carried a spiritual significance that would forever change the history of the universe.

Peace Through War

In this fallen world, where the weak are easily dominated by the strong, there will always be the need for some one to stand up and defend their freedoms. George Orwell said, "People sleep peacefully in their beds at night only because rough men stand ready to do violence on their behalf." Some liberators are able to emancipate the oppressed through diplomatic means. But there are times when only physical violence will achieve such goals.

Building a case for just war, English philosopher, John Mills, wrote:

War is an ugly thing, but not the ugliest of things. The decayed and degraded state of moral and patriotic feeling which thinks nothing worth a war, is worse. A war to protect other human beings from tyrannical injustice; a war to give victory to their own ideas of right and good; a war carried on for

41

*an honest purpose by their own free choice—is often
the means of their regeneration.*

In a fallen world, war is sometimes the only solution.
What did Biblical writers have to say about standing up for
those suffering beneath the heel of the oppressor?

Open your mouth (and your arsenal if necessary)
*for the speechless, in the cause of all who are
appointed to die. Open your mouth, judge
righteously, and plead* (strive for) *the cause of the
poor and needy.*

Proverbs 31:8-9
Comments mine

One of the meanings for the word *plead* in the verse
above is "to execute judgment." This speaks of action taken
against the oppressors of innocent, helpless people. Now
read what Job had to say:

*I was eyes to the blind, and I was feet to the lame. I
was a father to the poor, and I searched out the case
that I did not know. (He didn't plead ignorance, and
look the other way.) I broke the fangs of the wicked
(that's warfare!), and plucked the victim from his
teeth (that's deliverance!).*

Job 29:15-17
Comments mine

As individuals, we are often given the authority and
responsibility to defend and support other people. Whether
we are a father who is accountable for his wife and children,
or a military commander with the charge of liberating an
entire nation from tyranny, the authority to fight and defend

is established.

While it is true that Jesus told His disciples to not resist an evil person, saying, "But whoever slaps you on your right cheek, turn the other to him also" (Matthew 5:39), He did not say that there are never times when physical restraint of evil is warranted. I personally understand Jesus' words to mean that if I am insulted or persecuted for being a good Christian or decent citizen—then I am to suffer the injustice without a violent response. Instead, I should do as Peter exhorted when he said: "If you are reproached for the name of Christ, blessed are you, for the Spirit of glory and of God rests upon you" (1 Peter 4:14).

Regarding one's personal well being, Paul said, "Repay no one evil for evil" He also said, "Dearly beloved, avenge not yourselves, but rather give place to wrath: for it is written, Vengeance in mine; I will repay, says the Lord" (Romans 12:14, 17, 19). I believe a key word in this verse is, "avenge not *yourselves.*" If someone acts offensively toward you personally, suffer the wrong without a violent response! But Paul also said, "If it is possible, *as much as depends on you,* live at peace with all men" (12:18). As far as it depends on you, live at peace with everyone. Indeed, we should never mistreat anyone. We are not to pick fights. We should ignore a wrong when it is leveled against our own person. We may be cheated, slandered or slapped for being who we are—and that's sometimes to be expected! We should seek to suffer the wrong in the wonderfully forgiving spirit of Jesus Christ, our Lord and Master. But we should never ignore the injustice done to the speechless, defenseless and downtrodden. There are times when God will warrant the use of force to stay the violent hand of the evildoer. But even then it must be done in the right way.

Beloved, someone can curse me, spit in my face, revile and even slap me, and I will do all I can to keep peace with them. As a Christian I do not have it in my heart to react violently. But if I am responsible for someone else's welfare, I may have to fight.

What if God has given me a charge to protect you? Should I stand quietly to the side and allow someone to beat, rape or murder you? I don't think so. If I did that, I would be grossly negligent in discharging my responsibility both to you and to God who put you under my care.

Someone argues, "But the early Christians stood in line, watching as their brethren went to their deaths, and they didn't do a thing to resist!" Correct. But does that mean that if you place your child in my care, and a stranger comes up and demands that I hand him over, that I should yield to him? Let's be realistic here. Use the common sense God gave you. If someone attempted to kidnap and harm your child, you would want me to do whatever was necessary to protect him, wouldn't you?

If you are still not convinced that a Christian sometimes has the right to fight evil with physical force, you will have to admit that Paul does place that responsibility on the governments of nations. He indicates that kings, governors, rulers, magistrates and law enforcement personnel are "God's ministers to [us] for good," and argues that they "do not wield the sword in vain, but are God's ministers— His avengers in some cases—to execute wrath on those who practice evil" (Romans 13:1-4; 1 Peter 2:13-14). Whether these ministers are the police officers and judges who work on a local level against lawless men and women, or are the armed service personnel who defend a nation's freedom from tyranny, God has given them the authority to wage a literal, physical war against evil, lawless people. Thank God for this authority; without them anarchy would sweep the globe.

The Lamb Will Bring Judgment

The Prince of Peace is yet capable of executing great violence on the heads of His enemies. Those who disagree with this statement may cite the twenty six verses in the Revelation that refer to Jesus as the Lamb of God. "Only one verse," they might add, "calls Him the Lion of Judah." Perhaps that's why many are too comfortable with Jesus. What do we have to fear from a lamb anyway? Lambs are soft and cuddly, innocent and gentle. Lambs are not very aggressive, and their bleat can hardly be construed as a roar. Ah, but wait! Even the Lamb has a wrathful side. Revelation 6:16 warns of a coming time when rebellious men will scramble to hide in the caves and cliffs from the fearful wrath of the Lamb of God!

Old Ravenhill said, "The world thinks it is done with Jesus Christ, but the truth is that He's at the end of the road for every man and woman!" Regrettably, Jesus will be revealed as Judge to many who meet Him on that dreadful day (John 5:22; Acts 10:42). As Judge of the living and the dead, He will take hold of history, and pour it out for all to see (1 Corinthians 4:5). As a man empties the secret contents of an enormous sack before his friends and enemies, so the Lord will bring to light every secret thought and deed piled up against the unrepentant. And because there is so little of the fear of God today, I think that even many Christians will be terrified when they stand before God. They will not be doomed to an eternity without Christ, but they will hang their heads in shame when they face up to the fact that they failed to live fervent earthly lives for Him. Do not think that all Christians die happy. If they've wasted time, talents and wealth on frivolous things, Judgment Day will embarrass them.

Earth's Final Peace

Let us not forget that our Lord is both tender and tough. Final peace will only come as a result of the tougher side to His nature. We will never fully realize peace without war—not as long as the Devil is around! Lord of Sabaoth—the Lord of Armies—will one day descend in mighty power to vanquish His foes, conquering them "with the breath of His mouth...and by the brightness of His coming!" (See 2 Thessalonians 2:8 and Revelation 19:11-16.)

If at the end of this age Jesus does not come as Heaven's Champion to eradicate evil, mankind is doomed to self-destruct. The problems confronting the human race in the decades and centuries to come would simply be too overwhelming. Despite all of its advancements in science and technology, the world is still too far behind to ever catch up. Isaiah's apocalypse reveals that "last days" humans will wring their hands in anguish, crying, "We have not accomplished any deliverance in the earth!" (Isaiah 26:18). Too much is stacked against us. Consider the following challenges facing mankind.

1.   Inexplicable new strains of diseases and blights, decimating human beings, crops and forests.

2.   A growing shortage of fresh water.

3.   Militant Islamic radicals bent on dominating the world through terrorism.

4.   The subtle leopards of communism, which have only changed their spots and will again leap to the center of the world stage.

5.   Massive shortages of food, and sweeping famines.

6.   The increasing occurrence and intensity of natural disasters around the globe.

7.   Angry, belligerent and vengeful principalities in heavenly places, who presently are stirring the world pot to

a violent eruption.

Beloved, our Lord *must* soon come as Heaven's valiant warrior! He must come establish His undisputed Lordship! Through violent battle, He will inaugurate the lasting peace the world longs for, and bring freedom to all those who love His appearing (2 Timothy 4:8).

You have received a commission from our Heavenly Commander-in-Chief to reach mankind with the power of the gospel before the final curtain closes. If you don't personally receive this mandate, you will fail Him! It is time for you to take up spiritual shield and buckler, and carry the fight to Satan in his own gates. Locate the lost and dying in your community, and work diligently to set them free. You are an anointed liberator, equipped to free men from tyrannical, demonic injustices! You are a warrior by blood!

4
Valiant in Battle

The history of failure in warfare can be summed up in two words: "Too late!" Too late in comprehending the deadly purpose of an enemy. Too late in realizing the mortal danger. Too late in preparedness. Too late in standing with one's friends. Too late in uniting all possible forces for resistance.[1]

These solemn words, spoken decades ago by American General Douglas MacArthur, suitably explain the purpose for this series on spiritual warfare. The timeless principles of warfare, as well as the reasons why some win and others lose in life's conflicts, apply to everyone, young and old alike. Owing to the savagery confronting the Church at the end of the age, it behooves us to heed MacArthur's words, and do all we can to avoid being "too late" in warfare.

Let us not disregard the deadly purpose and mortal danger posed by the enemy. His threats are genuine and backed with substance. His purposes are malignant, and if he cannot kill us outright, he will shackle our lives with discontent and misery. His aim is to murder our vision, passion, and everything else we need for a long and productive life. We must neither appease nor ignore his rancor.

49

Neither let us be slack in preparation. The world belongs to those who are conditioned by proper training. You can be perfected in your spirituality. You can become an expert in the use of your spiritual gifts. Prepare to advance in the things of God, but prepare to defend yourself as you do.

Let us also stand by our friends and allies. This is not the hour to be a loner. We mustn't separate from the Christians in our churches and communities, but rather unite all possible forces for the advance of the kingdom in this last hour.

A Standing Army

From God's very first covenants with men, the authority and anointing to combat evil has been of vital importance. Therefore, the Lord has always maintained a standing army among His people. From Abraham's gifted fighters, to King David's illustrious mighty men, Jehovah-Tsebaoth (The Lord of Hosts) has assembled and anointed His people to do exploits in His name.

Two thousand years ago, when Jesus accomplished His earthly mission through death and resurrection, God changed His army from a natural deportment to a spiritual one. He also equipped it with an enduring arsenal of spiritual weapons, staggering in their potential. The name of Jesus, the spoken Word, and the precious Blood of the Lamb, applied under a heavy anointing of the Holy Spirit, will produce explosions of almightiness wherever room is made.

The Sure Foundation

The finished work of Christ at Calvary has become the sure foundation upon which God's army stands. Indeed, at the cross, Jesus defeated principalities and powers ranged

50

against us, and handed them a crushing defeat. For that reason, we never fight the enemy *for a position* of victory, but always *from* one! Being seated together in heavenly places in Christ Jesus (Ephesians 2:6), we are a formidable and irresistible force in the earth. When we properly exercise our spiritual authority, no part of Satan's kingdom can withstand us.

Even so, the victory Jesus won at Calvary does not always demonstrate itself easily. There are opposing forces yet scattered around the globe, parading in glaring defiance to Jesus' claims. They are the nasty pockets of resistance that always seek to interrupt the flow of God's blessings to humanity.

This is where today's spiritual warriors enter the picture. Christ's victory *must* be enforced by a spiritually violent host of men and women who are determined to establish Jesus' kingship throughout the earth.

The Place of Faith

For deeper insight into the nature of this militant host of spiritual fighters, let us see what the writer of Hebrews had to say about faith's important role in the success of God's armies down through the ages. Although not every Old Testament saint was a soldier, many were, and faith was that with which God moved in concert to put them over in battle.

> *And what more shall I say? For the time would fail me to tell of [those]: who through faith subdued kingdoms...escaped the edge of the sword...became valiant in battle, turned to flight the armies of the aliens.*
>
> Hebrews 11:32-34

51

No doubt, the men and women listed in Hebrews' Hall of Faith were amazing people by God's power. But it was only through their remarkable faith that His power was able to accomplish what it did.

Were it not for the obedience prompted by his faith, Abram would have remained in Ur, rather than become the pioneer of a new land for a new people. He would have remained Abram, and never become Abraham, father of a multitude.

Were it not for faith, Moses would have lived and died as a badlands sheep-herder, and someone else would have been raised up to deliver Israel from Egyptian bondage.

Were it not for the obedience prompted by faith, the walls of Jericho would have remained intact, and the children of Israel would not have possessed their inheritance.

Were it not for the obedience prompted by faith, a harlot named Rahab would have perished in the rubble of Jericho's crumbling walls, and not been numbered among the people of God.

Were it not for their faith, Gideon would have remained a cowering farm boy in the land of his birth; Samson would have been devoured by a lion or massacred by vengeful Philistines; the three Hebrew boys would have been consumed in the flames of a massive Babylonian furnace; and Elijah would have been bitterly humiliated before 850 false prophets on Mount Carmel. But faith prevailed in each case! Such faith in any generation is crucial.

Charles C. Price made this comment concerning the power of faith:

Faith is living. It moves and operates, and sweeps the enemies of the soul before its irresistible march. Does one need all the faith in the world? No! One needs only as much as a grain of mustard seed, if it is God's faith! Then mountains will be removed.[2]

It seems that the key to victory in life is always found in the possession and use of genuine faith. Every believer is given a beginner's measure when born again; perhaps the mustard seed size. However, few really know how to use and develop this faith into a mighty force that will move mountains.

The Seven Dimensions of Faith

In his book, *The Worship Warrior,*[3] Chuck Pierce spoke of seven dimensions of faith that should regularly be exhibited in the life of the Church. Let me address each of them in this study.

1.   Chuck first speaks of *Historical Faith,* the kind that arises in one's heart as he hears or reads about what God has done in the past. The many testimonies of great miracles, revivals and awakenings of the past stir our passions and help us believe Him to do it again!

2.   Next he refers to *Saving Faith,* the kind by which men receive and rest upon Jesus alone for salvation. If one is truly saved, this is where it all begins. This is where a beginner's faith is first realized.

3.   *Temporary Faith* is the kind that springs up when the Holy Spirit quickens a person to believe or act upon a promise or word from God. However, this faith will not endure if it isn't protected and nourished by a steady flow of God's Word into the heart. For example: When someone

walks the aisle of a church, prays a sinner's prayer, but then fails to do those things necessary to spiritual growth, he will eventually fall away from the faith. Because temporary faith will not see him through life's many trials, he needs to develop the *abiding* faith that only comes as we "follow on to know the Lord" (Hosea 6:3, KJV).

4. *Supernatural Faith* is the kind that lifts one above and beyond natural faith, enabling him to calmly receive outstanding miracles and answers to his prayers. This kind of faith is what we know as "the gift of faith," as mentioned in First Corinthians, twelve.

5. *The War of Faith* is the next dimension of faith Chuck addresses, and is that which mounts up as one perseveres in worship, study, meditation and confession of the Word of God, in spite of the hardship Satan sends to discourage him. Through warring faith, we ascend to a high-level walk with the Lord, rising out of the valleys of carnality into the heights of a truly Spirit-filled walk. To me, this is the most mature faith, one that leads to the next two dimensions of faith, which are *overcoming faith* and *manifested faith.*

6. *Overcoming Faith* is the kind that lives, moves, and has its being in the countenance of Heaven. "In the light of the king's countenance is life" (Proverbs 16:15). Overcoming faith thrives in the radiance of Father's face. Overcoming faith also prospers in the sound of Jesus' victory at Calvary, and celebrates in the resonance of His glorious resurrection and ascension. All men and women of victory understand what it means to be identified with Him. As in Heaven, men and angels celebrate all Jesus accomplished for earth's ruined race, so on earth we hear it and join in!

Blessed are the people who know the joyful sound! They walk, O Lord, in the light of Your countenance.

Psalm 89:15

7. *Manifested or Glory Faith* is the final dimension of faith Chuck discusses, and is the faith in which we should all aspire to walk. Such faith has resided in the hearts of all notable world changers down through the centuries. Whether or not these saints were famous was unimportant. Manifested faith set them apart because a special "glory" was evidenced in their lives. Their strict devotion and obedience to Christ brought them into a greater grace for victory.

The glory faith in his life helped a Shunamite woman perceive that Elisha was a high-level prophet of God. Something unique and different set him apart from the other travelers who passed through her town.

Glory faith in the life of Smith Wigglesworth prompted two train passengers (Catholic priests) to fall on their knees before him, and beg for his prayer. They didn't know that he was a simple uneducated plumber; they simply responded to the powerful presence of God that resided in his life.

Glory faith, living in the heart of Welsh intercessor, Rees Howells, displayed itself in a cancer-smiting unction that liberated hundreds of people, and touched off revivals in many places.

Beloved, may we all seek God until we come to the place where glory faith demonstrates itself at every sharp turn in the road, on the jagged shore of every swollen river,

55

and at the base of every formidable mountain.

A Long Haul Faith

Every dimension of faith can be seen in the remarkable lives of those listed in Hebrews, eleven. For some, God's intervention was released suddenly, with undeniable displays of miraculous power. For others, it was not so conspicuous, but was there all the same, flowing quietly and steadily like a small mountain stream toward some distant ocean.

Abraham experienced victory only after years of counting God's word faithful, even when it looked like it wasn't.

Noah experienced victory only after laboring many decades on a huge wooden ark nobody could understand, and for which everybody ridiculed him.

These men were persistent! Theirs was a "long haul faith," the kind I wish to emphasize in the remainder of this chapter. A steady, quiet and persistent faith is what the Church needs most and desires the least in this hour of great trial and tribulation. We thank God for the sudden and astonishing displays of His power to deliver, but we also know He doesn't always intervene that way to end our seasons of warfare and hardship. However, we can rest in the fact that long haul faith will bring us to victory, God's way and in His time. Indeed, when one must persevere in faith before his desire comes to pass, the work will be much deeper and more enduring when it manifests.

The race is not to the swift, nor the battle to the strong...

Ecclesiastes 9:11

I never rely on my own ability to achieve victory in life; neither do I expect quick conclusions to every project upon which I fasten my faith. Confidence in myself never works, nor does the belief that all battles should end quickly. Such arrogance has never pulled me through the really hard times. Total reliance on the Lord alone is what has seen me through thus far, and I am convinced that it will see me through everything to come. Indeed, the race (as well as the battle) is not to the swift and strong, but only to those who have paced themselves with a marathon faith in Christ's Word, His timing and power.

Faith is a Law

The first thing we discover about faith—all faith—is that it is a law, a spiritual principle by which, sooner or later, we appropriate God's gracious provision. No one can access redemption's pearls without it. No one can take for his own, the covenant provisions of Calvary, by keeping the law through perfect obedience or by doing enough good works. However, they can appropriate them through faith in God's integrity and gratuitous provision. Indeed, the very principle of faith, when applied correctly, will activate the power of God on our behalf, accessing justification and redemption, as well as many other covenant blessings afforded by the Cross. A vital, living faith can supersede certain other laws that would bind us to purely natural lives. While such faith never does away with an existing law, it can set it aside for specific times and purposes.

Consider, for example, the laws involved in aerodynamics. An airplane flies when it obtains enough *lift* from its passage through the air to sustain it. When this lift is augmented by the *thrust* produced by the action of the propeller, the total is more than enough to offset the downward effect of *gravity* and the static effect of *drag*. The airplane is then able to move forward and upward through the sky.

It is important to stress, however, that lift and thrust do not eliminate the laws of gravity and drag; they only dominate them at specific times and for specific purposes. Nevertheless, when the laws of lift and thrust are cancelled, for whatever reason, the airplane will automatically and immediately succumb to the laws of gravity and drag, beginning a rapid and unpleasant plunge to the ground.

Faith, and the power that follows it, is an overcoming spiritual law that will dominate negative forces, even as lift and thrust dominate gravity and drag. But we must keep the force of faith turned on at all times.

How then do we apply the law of faith to life's situations? If faith is a law, then how do we enforce it? First, by being sure we have the genuine article. Faith is not simply one's mental ability to consider something done; rather, it is a calm assurance, born deep in the heart, that something is done.

I saw faith beautifully displayed in the uncomplicated perception of my oldest son, Bruce, when he was a seven year old. Bruce had wanted a pony for several months, and I had failed to find one for him. One day when he was asking me about it, I told him that if he wanted a pony bad enough, he was going to have to use his own faith to get one. Taking my instruction to heart, Bruce disappeared into his bedroom for about fifteen minutes. When he came back, I asked him if he had prayed for a pony. He answered that he had. Curious, I challenged him by saying, "If you prayed for a pony and received it by faith, then where is it? Surely I ought to be able to see it!" To this query, Bruce cheerfully answered, "God's gone to get it for me."

That pretty well explains it, doesn't it? If we truly receive something by faith, we take ownership of it even before we see it, and believe God's gone to get it for us.

If a trusted friend were to hand me the title deed to an automobile he'd recently purchased while visiting in a distant state, and then told me that he was going to fly out to get it for me, I would thank him profusely and begin rejoicing that I have a new automobile. I might not know exactly *when* he would show up with my car, but I would rest assured, knowing him to be a man of his word. You see, as long as I have the title in my possession, stating that I own the car, *then I own the car!* If someone were to ask me where the car was, I'd simply say, *"My friend's gone to get it for me."*

Do you grasp the principle here? When God tells us that we can petition Him for something, and receive it by faith, He is offering us the title deed. And when that something is a blessing already purchased in the atonement, then we *really* have the title deed, signed in Christ's own blood! When I need forgiveness, I lean hard on the promise of forgiveness I find in His Word. When I need healing, I recall how Jesus purchased health for me at the cross. I deliberately read the title deed and begin rejoicing. The promises found in His Word become "the substance of things hoped for, the evidence of things not seen" (Hebrews 11:1). I have received healing numerous times by applying this principle of faith.

Sickness and pain are very real. When they strike our bodies, it is not fun, and very often frightening. We are not like the mind-over-matter religions that say sickness and pain are not real. But neither do we lay down and accept them without a fight! We must come to terms with the fact that the Lord has handed us the title deed to our healing,

59

and it's based on the atonement. Accept your healing by faith, rejoice even though you cannot see or feel it, and trust that God has gone to get it for you. Apply this principle in every area of your life. Faith really does work!

Developing Your Faith

Faith is a grace imparted to our hearts by the Holy Spirit when we ingest the Word of God by either reading or hearing it. This grace may be imparted instantly, as when a *rhema* Word strikes our hearts, but in most cases it grows only as we set our hearts to attend to the *logos* Word in a systematic and consistent manner. In time, the *logos* Word will build a genuine and overcoming faith that will both move the hand of God, as well as dominate the negative laws arrayed against it. Note the words I underline in the following verses from Proverbs 4:20-22:

> *My son, give attention to my words; incline your ear to my sayings. Do not let them depart from your eyes; keep them in the midst of your heart; for they (my words and the faith they impart) are life to those who find them, and health to all their flesh.*

Genuine faith comes when our hearts ingest (take in), digest (break down), and assimilate (absorb and incorporate) the precious Word on any subject relating to God's promises. As wholesome physical food must be digested and absorbed to maintain the life and strength of our physical bodies, so the Word of God must be digested and absorbed to maintain the life, strength and faith of our hearts.

> *Your words were found, and I ate them, and Your word was to me the joy and rejoicing of my heart;*

for I am called by Your name, O Lord God of hosts.
Jeremiah 15:16, NAS

When the Word of God is found and consumed by a hungry soul, spiritual joy and rejoicing are the surefire result. When we become thrilled with the truth we internalize, the power of that truth works effectively for us (1 Thessalonians 2:13). Therefore, when I need healing, I deliberately feed on the many promises concerning God's power and willingness to heal me. When I begin feeling old and worn out, I turn to the many promises concerning a long and productive life. When fear of financial failure and lack confronts me, I peruse the abundance of promises relating to God's faithfulness to care for me. When fear of harm rises up, I turn to all God says concerning angelic protection and covenant safety. As I do this, my heart is "strengthened with all might according to His glorious power" (Colossians 1:11), and life reclaims an exciting outlook based on a vital faith produced by the living Word. It amazes me to see what the Lord can do when I regularly vitalize my heart by feeding it the Word of God!

Applying Your Faith

When your heart has ingested, digested and assimilated the Word of God as it should, faith will become a vital force that can be applied effectively by calmly calling forth (not screaming out) what you want to see happen. In Mark 11:22-23, Jesus assured us that the God-kind of faith, born deep in one's heart, will be applied through words spoken from the mouth. If we never say anything, nothing much is going to happen for us. Faith statements, decrees and thanksgivings, which are based on a solid foundation of Scriptures, will help generate the power to turn negative things around, as well as procure the manifold blessing of God.

Faith: A Strong Wrench

Besides being a spiritual law, faith is also like a strong, drop-forged wrench, a tool to be used where a lot of pressure is required. When applied doggedly to stubborn situations, the force of faith, or, the power that faith activates, will prevail!

A few weeks ago I needed to remove a large nut from the side of one of my farm tractors. The nut was rusted on a bolt and wouldn't budge when I placed the appropriate box-end wrench on it and applied pressure. Rather than give up and leave things as they were, I squirted a healthy dose of WD-40 on the nut, and allowed it's rust-dissolving chemicals to soak in. That's like squirting a large dose of Holy Spirit anointing onto a stubborn situation and letting it work. Faith needs the power of the Holy Spirit in order to work effectively; in fact, faith without the response of God's power is useless and limits us to natural outcomes.

After allowing the WD-40 to penetrate the rust for a few minutes, I slipped a four-foot pipe over the handle of the wrench for added leverage and bore down with all of my might. Suddenly, there was a loud pop, and the stubborn nut broke loose from its frozen grip on the bolt. I was then able to remove it the rest of the way with my fingers.

Isn't it good to know that God has not left us without the proper tools for tackling difficult situations. The faith we have is like a sturdy wrench, but it must be fitted to the problem. If we don't fit faith to the problems of life, then we will never be those who snatch success from the jaws of defeat.

I am not exactly sure what the four-foot pipe represents, but I know it is whatever God gives us for more leverage against a problem. It may be the agreement prayer of other believers, or it may be the additional dynamic of praying and worshiping in the spirit (Jude 20).

Endurance: Maintaining Your Cool

When things don't give way as quickly as we would like them to, we must exercise the godly fruit of endurance (patience) and not readily concede defeat. A rusty nut will yield *if* we work at it long enough.

I had an old friend who lived down the road from my house a few years ago. He was recognized as the best heavy equipment mechanic around, and folks often said that if he couldn't fix it, it couldn't be fixed.

One day I asked him what he did when he ran into a problem that stumped him. "How do you keep from losing your cool, busting your knuckles, and giving up?"

"Instead of losing my temper," he answered, "I just lay down my tools, go to the house, and enjoy a cup of coffee out on the front porch. And then when I return to the problem, I have a better attitude, am more at ease, and the answer always seems to be waiting there for me."

My friend overcame his problems, not by fretting and losing his cool, but by patiently enduring the period of perplexity until he had the remedy he needed for his mechanical problem. Faith always works best when supported by such patient endurance. Patience will not allow you to pull your faith from the rusty nut when it seems it's not working, but keeps it there until God's power comes through again.

Endurance: The Supporting Infrastructure

Patience also acts like the supporting infrastructure that under girds the spans of a bridge stretching over a raging river. Without this infrastructure in place, holding and supporting the weight of the bridge and all that travels over it, the whole thing would fall into the river and wash away. That is why, when facing a trial of faith, James exhorted us to "let patience have its perfect work" (James 1:4). Indeed, the task assigned to patience during a trial is that of supporting faith until God's power comes through. No matter what we face, if we will give God's Word the time it needs to work, we will see our faith prevail consistently throughout our lives.

Embrace Your Patience

I recently heard a lady blurt out the words, "I don't have any patience! I'm the most impatient person I know!" With such a statement coming from her mouth, her faith will win few of life's battles. Rather than support the faith she has, she consistently undermines it. Instead of claiming to have no patience, she ought to be embracing it, and confessing, "I have great patience, and it's having its perfect work in my every trial!"

As a fruit of the Holy Spirit, patience resides in our human spirits, so let it work! Jesus instructed us, "By your patience possess your souls" (Luke 21:19). The application of this spiritual force will hold us calm even when all hell is raging against us. Instead of losing our minds to fear and worry, patience will keep us cool, calm and collected, allowing both faith, and God's response to it, the opportunity needed to accomplish amazing things.

As we begin a study of Israel's warriors and armies, let us not forget the common denominator enabling them to do the exploits we marvel at today. In all generations, the force of faith is the tool with which we overcome the indomitable, obtain the unattainable, move the immovable, and achieve the impossible. Indeed, the power of faith is a world dominator. "And this is the victory that overcomes the world—our faith" (1 John 5:4).

ENDNOTES

1. Edward Rice, Jr., *General Douglas MacArthur,* Dell Publishing Co., Nye York, N.Y., 1942, p. 18.
2. Charles S. Price, *The Real Faith,* Logos International, Plainfield, N.J., 1972, P. 39.
3. Chuck C. Pierce, *The Worship Warrior,* Regal Books, Ventura, CA. 2002, pp. 112-116.

5
Guardians of the Bride

Who is this coming out of the wilderness like pillars of smoke, perfumed with myrrh and frankincense, with all the merchant's fragrant powders? Behold, it is Solomon's couch, with sixty valiant men around it, of the valiant of Israel. They all hold swords, being expert in war. Every man has his sword on his thigh because of fear in the night.

Song of Solomon 3:6-8

The Song of Songs gives us a vivid description of Solomon's impressive wedding couch as witnessed by the daughters of Zion when sixty valiant warriors emerge from the wilderness, carrying the bride their king had called from a distant place. A wedding couch, or litter, was a portable seat in which royalty reclined when traveling from place to place. It had curtains on each side, which could either be drawn back or closed according to the wishes of the important person(s) within. At the four corners of Solomon's litter were several strong men (possibly two at each corner) steadying it on their shoulders, or perhaps carrying it in strong hands at their sides. As they passed through the wilderness, fifty-two other armed attendants jogged before and behind them, keeping attentive eyes on the landscape, ready to encounter and eliminate any terror (man or beast) that might come out of the night. And notice: they were valiant men—the most courageous in Israel! One version

67

calls them "the heroes of Israel." Perhaps a few years earlier some of them had been young mighty men under David's command as he steadily subdued the enemies that resisted his right to Israel's throne.

These noble warriors could handle the sword with great authority and skill, and were all elite combat veterans. Each carried a glory that made him look like a pillar of smoke slipping quietly through the wilderness. One translation describes the individual components of the group, together appearing as "pillars of smoke." Another translation describes them as one single entity, appearing together as "a column of smoke." Indeed, their appearance as pillars depicts the *individual* glory and anointing that rested on each warrior, while their appearance as a column depicts the *corporate* glory and anointing they carried as a whole. A Spirit-empowered believer is mighty when alone, but when he pulls together with other Spirit-empowered believers, mingling his spices with those of others in the mixing bowl of corporate worship and service to Jesus, the strength of glory and anointing is increased exponentially! In the New Testament, nothing ever shook when a lone individual prayed or worshiped God, but twice in the Book of Acts, buildings shook violently when believers put individual dynamics together. (See Acts 4:31 and 16:25-26.) And so, an awesome anointing and glory rested on Solomon's train of warriors as they carried him and his bride quietly through the wilderness with Jerusalem as their destination.

The escort was also comprised of wilderness-trained men—rugged outdoorsmen who knew the secrets of survival in a harsh and dangerous land. Undoubtedly the king placed great confidence in them, knowing his bride would be safe in their care. These men knew where the watering places were. They knew what ridges and canyons should be avoided, and where the lair of the lion was. They could look at the sky and determine what the weather would do for several days in advance. Truly, they were rugged men—capable and responsible heroes in whose hands the king could place precious lives.

King Jesus seeks such warriors today, men and women worthy to carry His couch—the glorious gospel—through the wilderness of this fallen world in search for souls who would become part of His eternal Bride. Such warriors are worthy bodyguards, responsible for protecting the Church from error, cunning wolves, and from the many snares Satan devises to captivate and destroy the people of God. They are not worthy because they have somehow earned their salvation (for that comes by grace alone), but they are worthy to carry the gospel through the darkness because they have given themselves to the training necessary to be effective shepherds. Like Paul, they have been anointed, counted faithful, and placed into important ministries (1 Timothy 1:12). They are eligible because they are given to higher ideals of godliness and service than are most believers. They know it is an honorable thing to be chosen and placed among those who escort the espoused to Christ. Each is properly trained in survival warfare and faithful stewardship. Each is spiritually perfumed with myrrh, frankincense and the merchant's fragrant powders, so that he might be both effective and attractive in his reasonable service.

Myrrh represents the fragrance of Christ upon us, which becomes the aroma of life to many who encounter it, and the aroma of death to others. Some find the sweet smell of Christ to be desirable, while others are offended by it, and thus reject the Lord of glory. (See 2 Corinthians 2:14-16.)

Frankincense represents the beauty and loveliness of Christ in our lives, as well as the fragrant love and worship

69

of those who passionately adore Him. A person will never be an effective carrier of Jesus' gospel who is not a passionate worshiper of God.

The merchant's fragrant powders represent the gifts and the fruit of the Holy Spirit in the lives of God's servant/warriors, and the swords strapped to their thighs represent a readiness to engage an enemy at a moment's notice. The sword also represents the power and authority to wage war in behalf of the King and His Church.

Solomon's palanquin, or bridal car, was an impressive work of art, made of imperishable cedar—white and pure—from the grand forests of Lebanon. In like description, Christ's couch is an everlasting gospel, not corroded by the hostile elements of the world. Indeed, the foul weather of changing opinions and rotten attitudes don't affect, even slightly, the soundness and purity of this glorious gospel.

Solomon's palanquin also had pillars of silver, representing the redemption we have through Jesus' sacrifice. Its bottom was made of pure gold, denoting the divine element of the couch, which is basic to everything we do in the Kingdom. Its seat was covered with purple, denoting the royalty of the king to whom the Shulamite was betrothed. Hence the Church is a royal priesthood, the beloved of Heaven's King, escorted by ministers of nobility and resolve.

How is it with you, beloved? Can you see yourself as a guardian of Jesus' cherished couch? Will you carry the gospel of Christ, gather up His beloved (all who will be saved), and usher them safely through the treachery of this dark world toward the Kingdom of Heaven?

Through the perils of this present darkness, we are to escort the Church through every hazard and "present [her] as a chaste virgin to Christ" (2 Corinthians 11:2). Hence, we must be valiant warriors—bodyguards willing to fight to the death any enemy that would seek to hijack the King's litter! Many are called but few are chosen for this important task, but only because they are not submitted to the training required by the Spirit of God.

Many years ago my wife and I realized that our primary responsibility on earth was to escort to Heaven as many people allotted to our charge as possible. With all the pitfalls designed by Satan to lead astray and captivate God's elect, we knew that they would need our encouragement and leadership over the long haul. This has required that we know the members of the flock as individuals and not just numbers. It has also required that we be dauntless with God's standards, regardless of who we face or how much pressure comes against us to bend the level for the sake of those who want to compromise the truth.

Beloved, revival warriors must be valiant for the truth! Revivalists must stand by the Word of God if they will have it stand by them. God is calling us to pit bull tenacity where His Word is concerned, and if we will face each situation with what He shows us in the Bible, we will stand separate and strong as the time of the end approaches.

The Bride's Escort

Slipping through the wilderness
Of worldly pain and mournful squalor,
Guardians keen, of gentle might,
Exhibit hearts of fervent love.

Sweet-scented myrrh and fragrant resin,
Valiant men from near and far,
Bold in war yet strong in mercy,
Loyal to their King above.

Devotion in their hearts a plenty,
Valor in their eyes ablaze,
Mission-minded and determined,
To honor King throughout their days.

Bracing couch in hands well-seasoned,
Bearing bride and bearing sword.
Vigilant and well-protective,
Defending couch of Gospel love.

And if from darkness danger threatens,
They'll not wonder what to do;
Rising up in gospel power,
They'll defend the truth for you.

So gathering now the souls from nations,
Reaching men for Heaven's cause,
Soon the day of Jesus' wedding,
Hour of gladness, hour of love.

— M. H.

Can you hear what the Lord is saying? It is an edict for you who would take the gospel couch into hand, and gather the end time Bride. It is a word to stir and encourage your heart for the action God requires at this particular time.

Rally your passion, My servant; step forth, bow low, and receive this mantle for souls! The hordes of darkness shudder to think that you are coming. Armies of evil will turn aside as you pierce realms where they've run riot. Resplendent in My glory you will blaze like a thousand suns, Yea, the thunder of a thousand guns will sound with each bold step you take, and devils will reel like fearful drunkards.

The prisoners await you, says the Lord, as they languish in cells of sin and degradation. But they mustn't wait for long, for this is the hour of deliverance; this is the hour of redemption glory!

As My servant-warrior, you possess the heart of the Breaker, even the heart of Jesus, Whose strong anointing He gladly places on your humble shoulders. So step forth, My champion, and break down the prison walls; break off the shackles that bind; break away the clammy hand of evil that pulls men down to death and perdition. Rescue those who would be My beloved, and transport them safely into My eternal Kingdom.

6
The Power of Choice

*Life does not give itself to one who tries to keep all its advantages at once. I have often thought morality may consist solely in the courage of making a choice.**

Many Christians become fruitless and frustrated in life simply by not making or following through with important decisions. Because they desire favor with everybody and malice from nobody, they restrict themselves and experience a monochrome existence. They cannot bear the fact that if they do anything of spiritual significance, or take a solid stand on any given issue, vicious critics will challenge and ridicule them. Such Christians are usually dominated by spirits of fear or rejection, and dread doing things that might gain the disapproval of those they think matter.

But life is to be lived to the full, and in order to enjoy victory, one must be decisive, regardless of the stink it will cause among a few contrary people. I for one am determined to make my life count for God, and I don't care a flip what anybody says about it! Before the Lord alone will I stand or fall on Judgment Day. My critics will not be there, neither will the detractors who today try to pull me from my destiny.

What Does the Word Say?

And if it seems evil for you to serve the Lord, <u>choose</u>

75

for yourselves this day <u>whom you will serve</u>...but as
for me and my house, <u>we will serve</u> the Lord!
Joshua 24:15

I call heaven and earth as witnesses today against
you, that I have set before you life and death, blessing
and cursing,; therefore <u>choose life</u>, that both you and
your descendants may live.
Deuteronomy 30:19

I have <u>chosen the way of truth</u>; Your judgments I have
laid before me.
Psalm 119:30

Curds and honey He shall eat, that He may know to
refuse the evil and <u>choose the good</u>
Isaiah 7:15

Moses... <u>choosing</u> rather to suffer affliction with the
people of God than to enjoy the passing pleasures of
sin.
Hebrews 11:25

The power God gives us to make many of our own
decisions is clearly established in Scripture. The Lord does
not predestine everything that happens in our lives. Many
difficulties in life are the result of foolish decisions, while
many blessings are the result of wise ones. Being, as He is,
outside of time and history, God certainly knows the
outcome from the beginning of our actions, but He does
not always determine it. We should not view life's
happenings like the young rock climber who challenged
the face of a cliff one day. Before he had climbed ten feet,
his foot slipped away from a shallow crevice, and he fell to
the ground with a thud.

"Whew," he said, as he staggered to his feet bruised and bloodied, "I'm glad that's over."

The young climber evidently believed that God was the one who orchestrated his fall that day, and that it was destined to happen; but perhaps if he'd been listening, he would have heard the Lord whisper, "Don't put your foot into that crevice," or "Don't climb that cliff, you dummy!"

Witnesses Against Yourselves

When Joshua instructed the children of Israel to choose whom they would serve—the gods of the Amorites, or the God of Abraham, Isaac and Jacob—they unanimously chose to serve the Lord. A few moments later, Joshua said to the people, "You are witnesses against yourselves that you have chosen the Lord for yourselves, to serve Him" (Joshua 24:22). What he said to each of them was this: "If you ever try to blame anyone other than yourself for the outcome of your life, the decision you've made today will stand as a witness, that *you* made your choice and were willing to live with the consequences, good or bad."

If a little boy's daddy decides to go out with his buddies every Saturday night and get drunk, his little boy will suffer terribly in the long run, in more ways than one. His daddy's decision to sow to the flesh will reap corruption in his family. Such results are never the will of God, neither are they predestined by Him! They are, however, the will of Satan, and greatly please him.

On Judgment Day, when the books are opened (Revelation 20:12), and every man and woman is judged by the things written in the books, each foolish and selfish decision a person made that produced horrible results will rise from the books to testify against them. That is why it behooves us, beloved, to make decisions today that honor and glorify the Lord.

Choosing to be Effective and Useful

Many sincere Christians erroneously believe that unless God sovereignly chooses to robe them with mantles of power, they are destined to lead run-of-the-mill lives of mediocrity. They have the idea that great men and women only come about because God makes them that way. While that is true in one sense, they also must realize that every powerful Christian has had a part to play in his own greatness. Each had to make decisions that contributed to his effectiveness in God's command—decisions that only he could make.

Too many believers leave it up to life's negative circumstances to make important decisions for them. Others relinquish crucial decision making to their flesh—the old man who wages war against the soul. Still others allow demonic influences to dictate their effectiveness in Christ's kingdom. People like these never seize God-ordained destinies. People like these never take dominion by decision. This produces a grievous result, in that wrong responses to God's offers of grace and power short-circuit the flow of His blessings in and through our lives.

The great missionary to China, Gladys Aylward, refused to allow circumstances to keep her from responding to the love-burden boiling in her heart for the Chinese people. Without an ounce of support from mission societies, she embarked on a journey that traversed Russia's harsh expanse, pierced the frightening terrain of Mongolia, and situated her in the land of her dreams. Had she been like the majority of Christians through the centuries, she would have allowed the lack of human support to stop her, and scores of Chinese souls for whom Jesus died would have been lost forever. Gladys Aylward took dominion by decision!

Taking Dominion by Decision

When arthritis plowed into my life over thirty years ago, I could have resigned to the life of misery that was forecast by the medical profession. But Jesus showed me another possible outcome: "According to your faith let it be to you" (Matthew 9:29).

By choosing to take the sword of the Spirit, which is the Word of God, I developed my faith into a dominating force that could stand against the desires the enemy had for my life. When the promise seemed delayed, and the pressure to quit was great, I persevered because I had decided to partake of the Lord's provision regardless of what it looked like or how I felt.

When circumstances and a lack of formal training rose up to discourage me from pursuing a teaching ministry, I simply decided to take God at His word and "make disciples of all nations" (Matthew 28:19). Beginning with people who lived in my small farming community, I began a Bible study that eventually became a church that eventually became an outreach to the entire world. I am so glad I chose to follow the leading of the Spirit so many years ago. The power of choice is truly amazing. One seemingly small choice to obey God can unleash a flood of glory and power on an entire region and around the world.

ENDNOTE

* Leon Blum, *Bartletts Quotations*, Little, Brown and Co., Boston/Toronto, 1980, p. 736.

7

The Special Forces Christian

Many believers act as though God has a special anointing gun in Heaven, and that He periodically chooses some lucky, unsuspecting soul on earth and anoints him for splendid service. However, this idea is not in good keeping with either Old or New Testament teaching.

While it is true that God has elite servants within the ranks of His massive spiritual host, it is not true that only those predestined to greatness get to be included in that special number. You have something to say about that, and so have I.

If you want to be an elite revival warrior, one through whom God can unleash Heaven's power on earth, then this chapter is for you. It was written to stir, encourage, and to give you a clear understanding of what is available to you in the final moments of this age.

The very word "elite" suggests the idea of aristocracy—government by the rich and for the rich. It carries with it the idea of inherited wealth and social position. I envision the wealthy aristocrat who never has to rub elbows with society's peons. After all, he's above them and better than they are, and to mingle with them would somehow diminish his dignity. However, this *is not* what we are talking about when we speak of the elite of God. Rather, we are speaking of the choice part—the most carefully prepared part of God's

81

enormous spiritual army. We refer to those servants who, like Joshua and Caleb, are of a different spirit than the rest of the pack. Not content to live in comfort zones with every one else, they run courageously ahead into all the Lord is doing at the vanguard of His plunge into enemy territory. Like the warriors of Zebulun and Naphtali in Deborah's day, they "jeopardize their lives ... on the heights of the battlefield," or as one paraphrase says, "in the hot places of battle" (Judges 5:18).

There are those in every army who are the most likely to succeed in dangerous situations. They always seem to be in the thick of what is happening and lead lives of great spiritual adventure. They are the intercessors and evangelists who swarm into the Church's hottest battles against the forces of darkness, and wrest human plunder from Satan's grip. They are the best, most courageous and trustworthy of all God has to throw at the enemy. But what makes them so different? Are they born to such greatness? Absolutely not! They are simply those who have given themselves to intense spiritual training, preparing long and hard to better serve the King whom they love.

Training Hard to Become the Best

In many books and motion pictures, we have been introduced to some of the most distinguished fighters mankind ever produced. They were highly trained experts in all kinds of warfare—particularly unconventional methods of warfare. Special reconnaissance, hostage rescue, and rapid assault were their forte. They could drive anything, fly anything, blow up anything, and accurately utilize whatever was placed in their hands. They were fighters of uncommon physical and mental caliber, experts in top-secret ground, water or air based operations. They were light infantry warriors, guerrilla warriors, and sudden strike warriors. Attacking by land, air or sea, they did things ordinary soldiers could not do. Lieutenant General Bill Yarborough aptly explained that "there are some itches that only Special Forces can scratch." With designations like Marine Expeditionary and Force Recon Units, Army Green Berets, Rangers and Delta Force, Navy Seals and Super Seal Teams, and Air Force Special Ops, they projected an aura of invincibility that emboldened their comrades and horrified their enemies. There seemed to be an otherworldly element about each of them—almost a super-human quality of the highest order, and we marveled at them.

Whether such warriors are simply the fictional characters we've seen in films, or whether they are the real life commandos who defend our nation's interests, they command our highest respect. Each of them has trained hard to become the best that they can be, and for an enemy to become the target their fury is woeful. They are at all times ready for rapid deployment, perfectly prepared to engage an adversary and grind him to powder.

The world was amazed at the effectiveness of American and British Special Operations Forces during the liberation of Iraq in the spring of 2003. During that war, military analysts often highlighted three major battlefronts set against the capital city of Baghdad by marine and army regular infantry. But they also spoke of a fourth, unseen front that was in place, operating by stealth and deadly accuracy, far ahead of the regular ground infantry. The combatants on this fourth front were comprised of the lethal hit and run raiders who are so high-tech and secretive, that the enemy was constantly perplexed as to their whereabouts and deadly activities. Gathering and relaying crucial information to their commanders enabled the army, navy, air force and marine ground and air artillery components to pinpoint and destroy targets of great importance with little collateral damage inflicted on innocent civilians or to Baghdad's municipal infrastructure.

One of the most thrilling feats performed by these furtive specialists, was the daring rescue of wounded nineteen year old army private, Jessica Lynch, from a heavily armed Iraqi hospital where she had been held since her capture several days earlier.

Under cover of night, the united efforts of Marine, Army, and Navy Special Ops Forces were able to sweep in and liberate Jessica, and get her out of Baghdad to the safety of her own people. Brilliant! Brilliant! Brilliant! Our hats are off to these guys, who like components of David's army, were "expert in war, with all weapons of war" (1 Chronicles 12:33).

I long for the day when elite ministry teams will infiltrate cities and regions throughout the world, locating and freeing those held captive by Satan. I long for the day when the despots ensconced in these nations will be of little significance, and that soul-winners will go for souls regardless of who holds political power!

In the 2003 war with Iraq, it didn't matter that Saddam Hussein and his generals wielded control in Iraq before America's main infantry units arrived at the nations borders. Marine Recon, Navy Seal, and Delta Force units had already infiltrated the country and were doing their job in spite of the blowhard threats of the pompous Iraqi leaders.

Three Elements of Attack

In Special Operations terminology, there are three main elements involved in a properly executed rescue mission. They are surprise, speed, and violence of action. With these fundamentals always on the minds of the combatants,

American Special Ops Forces presently boast, according to some experts, a 97% success rate.

At times spiritual warriors must use these elements of execution. When once we have discerned the will of God concerning a ministry effort, there must be no hesitation or holding back in executing it when once we're underway: "Whatever your hand finds to do, do it with all your might" (Ecclesiastes 9:10). If we engage a high-level principality through prayer, fasting and with spiritual decree, we must not let up until it has succumbed no matter how loud it's threats or how hard it's counter-attack. When going for souls in our communities, we must not have a start again, stop again, start again approach. It must be all or nothing at all. Examine more closely these elements of a properly executed rescue mission.

1.   Surprise: To strike with astonishment; to catch some one or some thing off guard.

Brilliant confederate general, Thomas "Stonewall" Jackson, held this philosophy for battle:

> *Always mystify, mislead and surprise the enemy, if possible, and when you strike and overcome him, never let up in your pursuit so long as your men have the strength to follow; for an army routed, if hotly pursued, becomes panic-stricken, and can then be destroyed by half their number.**

Over and over again, in his famous Shenandoah Valley Campaign, "Old Jack" successfully used this philosophy against three Union armies, striking where they least expected, and denying them the full resources of the Valley during the early years of the War.

I think many Christians reveal too many secrets

regarding their spiritual plans, allowing the enemy to set up resistance to the fulfillment of those plans. Beloved, mystify the enemy! Make him guess what your next move will be rather than be the one wondering what his next move will be. If you have an idea for advancing God's kingdom, do not broadcast it for every person or demon in your region to hear. Take thorough counsel with the God of Battles as you consider a possible course of action; take counsel with your comrades if the ramifications of your activity will affect them, but see that they too understand the good sense of secrecy in carrying out those plans.

2.   Speed: The act or state of progressing rapidly; the velocity with which something moves.

When it is time to act for kingdom purposes, slothfulness and foot-dragging will not do. The commando who hesitates while attacking will not live long. The football lineman who hesitates when the ball is snapped will end up on his rear end. In today's battles for the souls of men and nations, the Church must move with determination and celerity.

3.   Violence of action: The physical force used to execute an action on an opposing force; often explosive and devastating.

In the movie, "Gods and Generals," the army of Stonewall Jackson displays violence of action against the reclining Federals at Chancellorsville. With ruthless resolve, Jackson and his men charge into the unsuspecting troops and rout them completely.

In today's epic battles with the forces of darkness, the Church must use spiritual violence to pluck the prey from satan's teeth. It must pray with force, worship with fervency, evangelize with determination, and confront demons with fearlessness. Anything less than this will not accomplish God's purposes.

Pacesetters

The unique skills developed by the elite warriors of the United States Special Operations Units are not only crucial for their own success in warfare, but they also benefit the regular army through the hand-me-down principle. For instance, many amazing capabilities and skills we now find among soldiers in the regular army, were first explored and developed by the Delta Force a decade or more ago. When a soldier leaves Delta Force and returns to a regular Ranger unit, he passes his knowledge on to the officers in that unit who, in turn, train the rangers under their command. This skill and training then gets filtered down to the men and women in the regular army, and in this way, the entire army is elevated to new heights of knowledge, accuracy and effectiveness.

Applying this principle spiritually, it should be no different in the army we call the Church. The apostles, prophets, evangelists, pastors and teachers, in their respective realms of authority, should equip the saints beneath them with the same proven knowledge and skills they've used effectively in past operations. Those they train should then build upon these skills in fervent prayer, evangelism, and disciple-making, letting their expertise filter down to others. Overall, the Church of the last days should be more knowledgeable, more powerful, and more effective than any preceding generation of believers.

The Need is Great

Beloved, why are we waiting? The Lord of Armies is offering each of us a commission in a Special Operations unit. Each Church should have at least one of these units infiltrating the surrounding community. Every small town should have several. A large city should have hundreds of them, all operating in citywide unit cohesion. Reaching the lost, feeding the poor, liberating the confused and deceived, and releasing hostages at every level of society, should be each unit's forte—it's spiritual M.O.S. (Military Occupation and Specialty). Perish the thought that we might settle for mediocrity in outreach when the excellent lies before us!

God is looking for a few good men and women who have the mettle—the grit—to fill these positions in ministry. Special ministry can only be filled by Christians who have spent sufficient time and energy in the school of the Spirit. God looks for those He can place in uncommon situations; those who will keep their heads when things go off-center; and those He can guide behind enemy lines in order to locate and liberate captives. Trained warriors know how to slip in and wreak havoc in Satan's camp for the glory of God.

My good friend, evangelist Shurby Long, and myself, held a series of meetings in a small eastern city a few years ago. Following the Friday night service, we took a tiny team of people to a local nightclub where drug traffickers were known to be rampant. Positioning ourselves on the street outside the club, we began to mingle with the patrons who were still arriving in good numbers. Although a few of them turned a deaf ear to what we were saying, many politely listened to the gospel we shared, and several prayed to receive Christ as their personal Lord and Savior. We were, as Finney said, building a chapel a yard from the gates of hell.

When it became apparent that no more patrons would be arriving that night (after midnight), we joined hands and pronounced a judgment on the establishment, commanding the spirits that oversaw the stronghold to release their grip and get out of town. Within a couple of months, the nightclub lost business and closed its doors.

Kingdom commandos can accomplish amazing things in a short period of time if they are truly committed to the work. By keeping their own eyes opened to the needs of their community, and by using informants, they can locate the souls who are lost, sick and bound, and destroy many works Satan has built up.

A man concerned for the health of his nephew informed me of his losing bout with depression. Later that day, while in prayer, the Lord laid it on my heart to visit him. When I did, he saw me as an angel of God, and was eager to receive Jesus as his Lord and Savior. As long as such precious souls are not already part of a strong local church, they should be viewed as open game. Spiritual commandos realize that the world is up for grabs, and that if they don't reach the lost with the gospel, someone else is likely to reach them with a lie.

Two-by-Two

When it comes to soul-winning, some Christians work better in teams of two. The practice of fishing for the souls of men with a believer of like precious faith and vision is wonderful. Together they can identify, pray for, and reach out to a potential convert. Once a rescue mission has been decided, the team of two should arrange for a visit with him, preferably in his home. Using ample tact and congeniality, they should seek a brief audience with the potential convert, doing their best not to make him feel threatened by their visit.

Once one of the two has successfully engaged the person in conversation, the other one (who now becomes the supporting disciple) should begin praying quietly under his breath, being sure not to interrupt his teammate unless asked to add something. Often, if the two begin preaching to a person, he will feel overwhelmed and put up defenses. Therefore, one disciple should do the lion's share of the talking until the person is brought to a decision.

If there are attention-grabbing children or pets in the home, the supporting disciple, without being too conspicuous, should do what he can to calm or occupy them, nullifying their effectiveness at hindering the outreach. There are reasons why Jesus sent His disciples out two-by-two, and maybe this was one of them. Perhaps this verse applies here: "Two are better than one, because they have a good reward for their labor" (Ecclesiastes 4:9).

Besides going into homes to reach souls for Christ, we sometimes go into hospital rooms, or into shopping malls, searching for those who are ready to hear the good news. As Special Ops believers, we need to use our imaginations and discover bold new ways to apprehend the lost.

Tracts

As a believer who constantly wonders about the spiritual condition of those around me, I carry a supply of tracts that can be used to say what I often cannot vocalize because of time restraints. For instance, the other day I was stopped by a man with a sign at a highway work site. As I waited for the pilot truck to come from the other direction and escort me through the work area, it dawned on me that I should offer my personal testimony tract to the man with the sign. Leaping from my vehicle, I darted over to where he was and said, "I bet you get tired of standing here all day, don't you?"

"I sure do." he replied, with a weary, I'm-going-nowhere-in-life expression on his face.

In the friendliest manner possible, I offered the tract to him, saying, "While you're standing here, maybe you'd like to read this little pamphlet...it's the story of my life."

With a curious interest, the man reached out and thanked me for the tract. I then returned to my car to await the arrival of the pilot truck. A few minutes later as I rode away, I was overjoyed to see the man pouring over the words to the tract, perhaps getting his first clear explanation of his need for Jesus. I was blessed with a tremendous sense of accomplishment knowing that I had done something to reach another soul for Christ. Perhaps all I did was plant a seed in his heart. Maybe I watered a seed someone else had previously planted. But then again, perhaps a few moments after I drove away, that man bowed his head to ask Jesus to come into his heart and take over his messed-up life. Only eternity will tell how many people have been nudged closer to Jesus through a well-placed tract.

Evangelist Mac Gober tells of an old black lady who knocked on his door one day in a courageous attempt to reach his kind for Christ. Mac, a free-spirit outlaw biker, was not home at the time, but his coarse roommate was. When the lady offered the tract to him, he smacked her in the face and ran her from their door with a barrage of curse words. A little while later when Mac returned home, he saw the tract lying on the floor, picked it up and started to read. God's message of love quickly seized his hard heart, reducing him to tears, and he was gloriously born again. In the years since then, Mac Gober has traveled the world, reaching souls for Jesus, and changing lives forever. He also founded a home for troubled boys that has helped hundreds of young men find their bearings in Christ. This one man, rescued by a valiant tract-carrying lady who was willing to suffer persecution for her witness, proves that tract ministry is a crucial and viable means of spreading the gospel of Jesus Christ. All of us ought to be using them!

ENDNOTE

*   Thomas J. Jackson, *Battles and Leaders of the Civil War,* Appleton-Century-Crofts, Inc., New York, N.Y., 1956, p. 195.

8
Rescue at Hobah

I simply love rescue operations. As a child, my favorite movies were those where the good guys defeated the bad guys and rescued those held captive by them. This is why I often reflect on the incident in Uganda, East Africa, in the late nineteen seventies, when dictator, Idi Amin, hijacked an Israeli airliner at Entebbe International Airport. This vicious ruler thought he'd won world respect by humiliating Israel in this way, but most of the world was appalled by his unwarranted behavior.

For hours the vainglorious despot gloated and ruffed his feathers like a cocky rooster as news of his catch made international headlines. But suddenly, in a lightning-fast rescue mission carried out by crack Israeli commandos, the hostages were seized and airlifted out of Uganda before anybody knew what was happening. Idi Amin must have been shell-shocked by this turn of events, for suddenly the world was laughing at him!

Raids like the one at Entebbe have been accomplished by anointed warriors since the very beginning of God's covenants with men. They are always dazzling displays of His military prowess operating through mortal men. And God has not changed. In this hour, He not only anoints the units of some natural armies for battle, but He also anoints and deploys *spiritual* commandos for cosmic battles with the powers of darkness. Jesus Christ leads these dynamic rangers, and as they keep their hearts and eyes on Him, He shows them exactly what to do in every trying situation. However, like the servants who comprised His special forces at other times, they first must be trained in the art of warfare. It has always been this way. Let us consider Abram's elite fighters.

Abram's Fighters

Early in the days of Abram's sojourn in the land that would become Israel, a confederation of wicked kingdoms headed by Chedorlaomer, king of Elam, attacked the area where his nephew Lot had settled. Lot and all he had were quickly carried north, to a destination beyond the crowded, bustling city of Damascus.

> *Now when Abram heard that his brother was taken captive, he armed his three hundred and eighteen trained servants who were born in his own house, and went in pursuit as far as Dan. He divided his forces against them by night, and he and his servants attacked them and pursued them as far as Hobah, which is north of Damascus. So he brought back all the goods, and also brought back his brother Lot and his goods, as well as the women and the people.*
> Genesis 14:14-16

Abram's action against the wicked kings who kidnapped Lot is the very first rescue mission recorded in the Bible. There are several interesting factors involved in this story that would be good to point out.

The first thing Abram did when he learned of his nephew's kidnapping was maintain his composure. Rather than strike out in a frenzy to save Lot, he took the time to muster his *trained* servants. This might have taken several

94

hours. Perhaps some of these special servants were a day's travel from Abram's home near Hebron and needed time to respond. Their master had the good sense to wait until he could pull them all together and arm them with the proper weapons. Too often, well-meaning Christians launch out to do big things before they are properly equipped. This can be very dangerous for them as well as for the people they involve.

The King James Version calls Abrams warriors his *instructed* servants. Proper instruction in warfare was essential. Not just any servant was qualified for a rescue mission of this magnitude, and only those with knowledge and the proper fighting skills could hope to be successful in such a dangerous undertaking.

Another factor worth highlighting is that each of Abram's fighters were *born in his household.* This means that they were no strangers to their master. Each servant's loyalty was certain; because Abram knew them from birth, and had supervised their training, he knew exactly what they could do in a combat situation. Other servants lived and worked in his household, but Abram used only his battle-trained servants to rescue his kinsman.

I think it important that pastors, and others in spiritual authority, not use just anybody who says they want to do something big for God. All leaders should reserve the right to examine a person's life before entrusting them with the authority to represent their church or ministry. How is the person's character? Do they conduct their affairs with integrity? How much knowledge and gifting do they have? Do they share your vision? Are they team players, or are they liable to desert you when things don't please them? When addressing the appointment of people to important roles, I think Paul's caution concerning the placement of deacons applies here: "But let these also first be tested; then let them serve as deacons, being found blameless" (1 Timothy 3:10).

Pressing the Fight

Abram and his warriors overtook Chedorlaomer's evil army at Dan and thrashed them all the way to Hobah, somewhere north of Damascus. Like Abram, we should see our battles through to the very end. Had he halted his pursuit between Dan and Hobah—possibly at Damascus—Abram's kinsman would never have been rescued.

I think that, too often, Christians let up in their pursuit of things precious to the heart of God. If it is the soul of someone needing salvation, they stop believing when they don't see a change that indicates that God is at work. When they need healing, they lose heart and recall their faith when they don't begin feeling better, or when the doctor's report is contrary to the Word of God. When called to press toward the fulfillment of their ministries, they sit down and pout when adversity rises against them. But beloved, if we will be warriors of special merit, accomplishing many things for God's kingdom, we must not be quitters, but with Paul, "press toward the goal for the prize of the upward call of God in Christ Jesus" (Philippians 3:14).

Battling the Enemies Within

Let us now examine the names of the three cities involved in this episode, and learn what we can from them.

Dan, the city where Abram first engaged his enemies, was in the northernmost part of Palestine, but south of Damascus. The name, Dan, in whatever usage, means "a judge." When Abram and his warriors came upon the evil kings at Dan, they began executing a form of judgment called war. Because Chedorlaomer and his confederation drew first blood, Abram was justified in judging and destroying them.

Damascus was the city north of Dan, which the evil kings likely passed through or around as they headed farther north to Hobah. The name *Damascus* means "activity." As the oldest city in that part of the world, it was an international trade city bustling with activity. Great caravans crisscrossed the land surrounding Damascus as people came and went for a variety of reasons. Certainly it was a place to confuse and distract Abram and his men from accomplishing their mission.

Hobah, the city north of Damascus, and that to which the evil kings fled, means "hiding place." Perhaps Lot's captors believed that if they could only make it to Hobah, they would find refuge from the fiery judgment Abram's warriors sought to bring upon their heads. But what happened? Abram and his warriors slaughtered the evil kings from Dan, right past the activity and commotion of Damascus, and straight into their hiding place at Hobah. Their mission was undistracted and thoroughly executed!

So how does this apply to us today? When I hear Christian people complaining about losing their peace and joy, or bemoaning the fact that they've lost their vision, passion or purpose, I realize that some evil kings have hijacked these precious graces and hauled them north to Hobah. Often these individuals blame demons or other people for their plight, but in reality, the works of their own flesh are to blame. Peter said, "fleshly lusts wage war against the soul" (1 Peter 2:11). Indeed, fleshly thieves like laziness and stubbornness are often the culprits who steal our peace and joy. If one is too lazy to draw near to God in sweet, on-going fellowship, peace and joy will be impossible to keep.

Internal enemies like strife and bitterness, or resentment and hatred, also may be blamed for a person's loss of vision, hope and purpose. Jesus said that the failure to forgive others for the wrongs they've committed will place us into the hands of the tormentors (Matthew 18:34-35). In this sense, the internal enemies residing in our flesh make room for demonic exploitation.

Some people surrender their hope for the future to the evil kings of self-rejection and self-hatred, never realizing that these two enemies cripple the flow of God's love in and through their lives. If we dislike ourselves, it will be difficult for us to love others as we should.

Other people lose anointing and favor to the inborn enemies of arrogance and an excessive self-love. No one receives easily from egotistical and self-focused men and women. While humility and a servant's heart attract God and men, pride and self-centeredness repulse them. Many brilliant and talented Christians remain unused today, simply because their prideful and arrogant self-opinion drives people away.

Paul readily admitted "For I know that in me (that is, in my flesh) nothing good dwells" (Romans 7:18). He knew that, lurking within his flesh, were the dream-stealers and thieves who could snatch away his present and becloud his future, and he wouldn't let them stay.

Stolen Emotions

Inborn enemies also hijack people's emotions, passions and sentiments that should be released freely through laughing, crying, rejoicing, dancing and through wonderful expressions of love. God wants us to feel deeply His love for us, and express freely our love for Him and our fellow man. But the innate kings of pride, fear and stubbornness won't allow us to do that.

As a pastor and worship leader, I have watched with sadness as certain people in my congregation have suppressed their feelings for God. I could see that they wanted to raise their hands in worship, but they wouldn't do it; I could see that they wanted to get out of their seats and dance in the aisles, but they remained in a state of spiritual paralysis; I could see that they wanted to shout "Hallelujah!" but inner enemies would not let them utter even a feeble word of praise. Our churches are filled with believers like these.

Then there are those people who have no problem expressing their emotions, but they often use their freedom to conceal another set of evil kings that lurk within them. Sometimes those who yell "Amen!" the loudest are the very ones with the deepest inner problems. They somehow think that if they can shout often enough, then people will think that they are spiritual and have it all together. But often these folks have a problem with submission to authority. They tend to be contrary, independent, and short tempered, comprising that puzzling breed of sheep who jump from church to church, and never really become a part of a team of people who are doing something significant for God. Rather than become living stones, set securely into the framework of a growing church, they are rolling stones, forever moving about, forever looking for the greener grass, and forever learning, but never able to come to the knowledge of the deeper set of truths that will free them from their wanderings. They may seem to worship freely, but inside they are bound up in a pitiful way!

When the evil kings fled north to Hobah, they slipped

through or around Damascus, the city of much activity and commotion, hoping that Abram's pursuit would end there. The enemies within us may be good at hiding behind a lot of commotion, but God is not fooled! When sin seeks concealment behind any kind of religious or secular activity (Damascus), it must be pursued and destroyed! Don't be fooled just because you praise well. Don't be conned by your reasonable-sounding excuses. Deal with the sin and laziness of your flesh, or all they have stolen will remain in their possession and you will never fulfill your destiny in God. You may look spiritual, sound spiritual and try to act spiritual, but the fruit you produce will be rotten!

I once knew a woman who put on quite a show when she attended church functions like prayer meetings and conferences. She could pray and prophesy with great emotion; she could dance and sing under what appeared to be a powerful unction; and she could make the casual observer believe she was very spiritual. But lurking deep within her were the evil kings of stubbornness and rebellion that never allowed anyone close enough to address the sin in her life. Her wanton behavior outside of church was atrocious, and everyone in the community saw her for what she really was, and disdained her witness. If she doesn't repent, Judgment Day will terrify her.

God Doesn't Need Our Sacrifices

The prophet Samuel scolded a pseudo-spiritual king named Saul, asking, "Has the Lord as great delight in burnt offerings and sacrifices, as in obeying the voice of the Lord? Behold, to obey is better than sacrifice, and to heed than the fat of rams" (1 Samuel 15:22). The foolish king had recently attempted to sidestep his own responsibilities as king by doing something "spiritual." This disobedience cost him the kingdom.

Beloved, passionate prophecy, praise and prayer are delightful offerings to give to the Lord, but only when we are seeking to abide by His moral and ethical standards as well. Christians everywhere pray fervently for revival, and that may be good. But as A. W. Tozer said, "Revival will [only] happen when prayer is no longer used as a substitute for obedience." Let us first be obedient to all God has spoken to us, then our prayers will count for something.

Undistracted and Determined

Much activity and commotion did not keep Abram from finding Lot in Hobah. His little army was not distracted by the din of Damascus. They pushed through or around it, cornered the enemy in Hobah, and rescued his kidnapped kinsman.

When it comes to snatching the prey from the jaws of evil, we must pursue our enemies past the religious commotion and whirring activity of our busy lives, and trail them right into their hiding places. We must deal ruthlessly with our own inborn enemies, as well as with the demonic powers that hold things in bondage. If it is demonic, cast it out! If flesh, crucify it! Often, in the very hiding place of evil, we will crush the enemy and liberate all he has in his grip. And realize this: Abram's warriors did more than simply rescue Lot. They wiped out the enemy! When Abram returned from the battle, Melchizedek, the priest and king of Salem, received a tithe of all the plunder he had taken from the dead bodies and ransacked camps of the evil kings. The writer of Hebrews called it a slaughter (7:1).

Executing the Kings

There are several practical things we can do in order to execute judgment on the evil kings in our flesh, and recover all that they have stolen. Like Abram, we can recover all! We can rescue our hope, revitalize our vision and passion, and reclaim a wonderful sense of purpose in life. Let us settle for nothing less.

1. Be honest with yourself. Once an enemy has been identified, admit that it has been working against you, and begin executing judgment at Dan. Paul said, "For if we would judge ourselves, we would not be judged" (1 Corinthians 11:31). Once the battle has begun, don't allow Damascus to hide your sin. Drop a lot of secular activity and discard religious show until you can get to the root of your problem and execute the evil kings.

2. Obey the Scriptural injunction to "overcome evil with good" (Romans 12:21). When the temptation to yield to an inborn evil arises, take the good Word of God that stands contrary to it and confess it aloud! Overcome the desire of the inner enemy with the Word of God.

A sister recently confessed that her own familiar enemy was self-hatred. Things she had done in life embarrassed her, making her feel lower than low itself. We told her that if she had repented and stopped doing those things that were wrong, then she could make a stand on the Word and reclaim her sense of acceptance and wholeness. Each time her flesh or a demon would remind her of how despicable she was, she would counter with a barrage of Scriptures proclaiming God's unconditional love for her, and how valuable she really was to Him. In a short period of time, she won the victory over self-hatred and reclaimed her joy.

3. When you are tempted to yield to the evil kings within your flesh, deliberately rebel and do the very opposite of what they tell you to do. When laziness tugs at you, begging you to stay in bed for several more minutes, force your mind and body from the comfort of your covers and get into the Word and prayer. When resentment or anger encourages you to do something spiteful to someone who has offended you, go out of your way to do something nice for them. When stubbornness and rebellion give twenty reasons why you should leave the church God has called you to, get as close to your spiritual leaders as possible and do twenty things to serve them. When pride rises up and encourages you to take offence at something said or done, make yourself into the humble person upon whom God delights to pour out His grace. Rebel against the dictates of the flesh!

4. Stay connected to the Vine. Jesus said, "I am the Vine, you are the branches" (John 15:5). He also said that the branches cannot bear fruit unless they remain connected to the Vine. The Holy Spirit working in and through us will overcome every negative influence in our lives if we will just stay connected to Jesus through His Word, prayer and worship.

5. Be connected and accountable to those around you, particularly those with whom you are called to serve, to those who know and love you. These people will often recognize when you begin yielding to the inner kings within, even when you do not. If they are true friends, they will speak to you about it, and if you are a true friend, you'll let them help you.

Jesus spoke of the need for the "branches" (plural) to abide in Him. I believe He was addressing the need for His disciples to be connected *together* as they abide in Him. Isolation from other Christians is never wise. I'll even go so far as to say that separation from the Christians God has called you to serve with is foolish. When you submit to live and work among the believers you belong with, a spiritual dynamic will be released that will strengthen everybody involved. Within a God-ordained connection like this, there will come the help we need to identify and eliminate our inner enemies and better produce the fruit of God.

6. Commit to a regimen of fasting. Nothing weakens inner enemies quite like targeted fasting. When recalling those times when he could have lost his destiny in God to the inner enemies of pride, rebellion and vengeance, David said, "I humbled myself with fasting" (Psalm 35:13). A program of regular fasting helps to sound the death-knell over the internal enemies that would carry your emotions, vision and destiny into captivity.

7. Walk in the Spirit, and you will not fulfill the lusts of the flesh. Rather than going over your list of don'ts, try spending more time looking at your list of dos. Apply your mind and energies to serving the Lord in practical ways. See to the activities of the spirit and your enthusiasm for godly things will only increase. As you attend to the Word, prayer, fellowship with your brothers and sisters, and service to God and man, your spirit will ascend to a higher position of strength than the enemies in your flesh. You will become so busy and fulfilled in the things of God, that you will have no interest in the activities and amusements that strengthen the inner enemies. "Walk in the Spirit, and you

shall not fulfill the lust of the flesh" (Galatians 5:16).

Participation the Goal

Remember, the Lord always sends disciplined servants on do-or-die missions. Lazy believers rarely participate in such campaigns because they haven't given themselves to the rigid training necessary to be effective. So they end up being like a big, strong kid in the bleachers who was too lazy and undisciplined to endure August's hot days of practice when the coach was deciding his lineup. Like this kid, they watch the great game being played out by their friends, but they watch from the bleachers. They may have the potential to be great champions, but because of laziness, or because of a preoccupation in trivial things, they have to observe the game from across the fence. Ask any athlete with the potential for greatness if such an experience is fun, and he will tell you it is not. He would rather be on the field winning than watching the game from the bleachers!

I was on the field immediately following a football game in which a local high school won its first ever state championship. As emotional and joyous as the celebration was, I could see the faces of a couple of boys in the bleachers who had missed their opportunity to play on the team. One boy had been too busy paying off a fancy car to be able to devote himself to the coach's rigorous schedule, and the other boy was too enthralled with a girl over in the next county. By the time the championship game arrived at the end of the season, the one boy's car had been irreparably vandalized, and the other boy's girlfriend had dropped him for another guy. And there they sat in the bleachers, watching their buddies grind out a gridiron victory in the most important game of their lives. To guys like these the victory

105

is always bittersweet. They may be happy that their friends won the game, but they are unable to share deeply in the thrill enjoyed as the trophy is hoisted over their heads in jubilation and triumph. No matter what anybody says in an effort to make them feel a part of the win, they know that the game was won without their participation, and it hurts deeply.

Beloved, as an ambassador for Christ, don't sit in the bleachers during this great contest for the souls of men. There is a position on the field for everyone who wants to participate. If you remain lazy, disinterested, preoccupied or untrained, you will find that you are useless to the King as He closes out this exciting Church age. But if you shake yourself from the dust of apathy and laziness, you will participate and experience the thrill of watching Christ vanquish His foes!

Get in the Game!

Dear friend, dare to get in the game. Get right in the coach's face and plead, "Play me, coach! Play me, coach!" When a wise coach sees that kind of eagerness in one of his athletes, he will work that player in somewhere! So get excited about spreading the gospel! Don't settle for mediocre Christianity. Ralph Waldo Emerson rightly said, "Nothing great was ever accomplished without enthusiasm." Life is too short to be shallow, and our years are too few to be boring. A person is never so alive as when he feels deeply, acts fearlessly, and attacks life with frankness and enthusiasm. May we heed Sir Winston Churchill's call to battle, but only to the spiritual fight that rages for the souls of men:

*Come on now all you young men, all over the world; you have not an hour to lose! Take your places in life's fighting line. Don't be content with things as they are. Enter upon your inheritance, and accept your responsibilities. Raise the glorious flags again, advance them upon the new enemies who constantly gather upon the front...and have only to be assaulted to be overthrown.**

ENDNOTE

* Stephen Mansfield, *Never Give In: The Extraordinary Character of Winston Churchill,* Highland Books, Elkton, MD., 1995, p. 85.

9
Integrity and the Warrior

For want of integrity among the children of Israel, "the men of Ai struck down about thirty-six men...and struck them down on the descent; therefore the hearts of the people melted and became like water" (Joshua 7:5). This account explains that the men of Ai struck the Israelites down "on the descent," typifying the downward spiraling condition of a people who lose touch with their integrity.

For want of integrity, a tormenting spirit was loosed on king Saul of Israel, filling his heart with trepidation and weakness. Later, when Goliath appeared on the scene to challenge his army each morning, the man who should have accepted the challenge, cowered in fear behind his own lines.

For want of integrity, David compromised the future blessing of his entire family line. When he arranged for Uriah the Hittite to be killed in battle so that he might take his wife for himself, David incurred a curse that denied him the blessing of peace and an enduring kingdom. His sin also gave a great occasion to the enemies of the Lord to blaspheme the God of Israel (2 Samuel 12:11-14).

Integrity in the life of God's spiritual warrior is imperative; in fact, imperative is not a strong enough word to describe its necessity. Scripture says that the Lord "searches all the earth for people who have given themselves completely to Him. He wants to make them strong" (2 Chronicles 16:9, TNCV). The Revised Berkeley Version says that He looks for those whose hearts are "full of integrity toward Him."

Although the promise of strength is a thrilling revelation of God's intention for His children, He seldom finds those through whom He can demonstrate this strength. Many are called to life in the supernatural flow of the Spirit, but because of a shortage of integrity, only a few actually experience it.

Properly defined, integrity means the quality or condition of being complete, whole, sound, upright, honest, humble and sincere. The very word implies that the man of integrity is scrupulous in all his dealings, and faithful to his commitments, his people and his God. Integrity allows for no compromise in important moral and ethical convictions. Integrity knows that, "Like a muddied fountain and a polluted spring is [the] man who yields, falls down, and compromises his integrity before the wicked" (Proverbs 25:26, TAB). Integrity receives no bribes, slanders no man, speaks the truth in love, and swears to its own hurt without changing.

The life of integrity is driven by three primary motivations; by three internal forces:

1. A genuine love for God and for fellow men.
2. A deep fear of God; a reverence that pervades one's entire being.
3. A strong desire to be useful to God.

Without these motivating forces in place, integrity will be in short supply and usefulness in God's kingdom will be hit and miss at best. So we can easily see that "integrity" is both a loaded term and inexhaustible subject. It all has to do with sound character. The man or woman of sound character is a man or woman of integrity.

Perhaps you've heard structural engineers refer to the integrity of a steel beam used as a support in a building or a bridge. If the integrity of the beam is sound, then it can be trusted to carry the weight they want to place on it. If its integrity is questionable, the beam must be replaced with one that is sure to be sound and trustworthy.

People are much like a steel beam. The Lord would like to place a lot of responsibility on us as He brings this age to completion, but all-too-often He finds stress fractures in our character that limit the amount of service we can render to His cause.

To be a man or woman of integrity means that you have proven yourself to be trustworthy. It means that your character is impeccable and your word can be trusted. A person of integrity is completely given to God, wholly devoted, unquestionably faithful in all his dealings. The Lord places such a high premium on this kind of character, that He measures it when selecting His students—and His warriors.

The humble He guides in justice, and the humble He teaches His way...Who is the man that fears the Lord? Him shall He teach in the way He chooses.
Psalm 25:9, 12

And the things that you have heard from me among many witnesses, commit these to faithful men who will be able to teach others also.
2 Timothy 2:2

111

There are many Christians who wonder why the Lord won't use them more than He does, and they are irritatingly frustrated. Their irritability makes life for family and friends almost unbearable as they blame others for what they've created themselves. It may be that they are not showing God the integrity He requires before promoting them. It may be that they have not shown themselves faithful to certain criteria God and their leaders have put in place as a proving ground for their character.

"But I am so talented and gifted for the work to be done!" one disgruntled church member grumbles.

Ah, but didn't you notice that the verse in Timothy said to commit the ministry to *faithful* people, not simply to *able* people?

How faithful are you to hang close to your spiritual family when things don't go your way? Do you gather up your marbles and go home? How faithful are you to sustain and affirm your comrades, to their faces and behind their backs, rather than tear them down? How faithful are you to pay your bills on time, or at least let your creditors know your good intentions are not just empty promises? How faithful are you at attending church workdays, prayer meetings, or ministry planning meetings? Your response (and attitude) concerning these things will promote or demote you in the army of God.

Integrity means everything to the Lord! Only those with "clean hands and a pure heart" will ascend the hill of the Lord! (Psalm 24:3-4). Only those who "walk uprightly, work righteousness, and speak the truth in their hearts" will dwell securely in the tabernacle of His presence (Psalm 15:1-2).

AIDS

In the prologue to his book, *The Death of Ethics in*

America, syndicated columnist, Cal Thomas, identified another malady called AIDS that is devastating American society, and I might add, the American Church. Not only do the initials "AIDS" stand for *Acquired Immune Deficiency Syndrome,* but they could also refer to what Thomas calls *Acquired <u>Integrity</u> Deficiency Syndrome.* "Although not life-threatening in the same way as the other form of AIDS," Thomas argues, "an integrity deficiency syndrome can subtly contribute to the decline of a culture in a way that will go unnoticed until it is too late."* This form of AIDS, like the other, will send an individual into a slow, steady decline.

The Benefits of Integrity

If there are serious negative consequences to a lack of integrity, there are also serious positive consequences to a great supply of it. The Old Testament reveals several such benefits:

1. Integrity protects and maintains.

Let integrity and uprightness preserve me, for I wait for You.

Psalm 25:21

Integrity is something that actually works to safeguard one's life from all the evil that lurks about. Never is there a time when the enemy does not circle our borders, seeking a breach through which to deliver his payload of destruction. Finite and limited as we are, there is no possible way we can guard all of our own borders, and so we need outside help. If we will walk in integrity before God and man, the Lord Himself will watch our borders for us.

113

2. Integrity fills one's heart with gladness.

*Light is sown for the righteous, and gladness for
the upright in heart.*

Psalm 97:11

Revelation and insight, gladness and joy, are worthwhile
remunerations that show up in the lives of those who are
upright in heart.

3. Integrity garners the Lord's strong guidance in life's
    diverse affairs.

The integrity of the upright will guide them.

Proverbs 11:3

Supernatural guidance is a wonderful thing to have. In
the life of the warrior it is critical. The minefields of Satan
are multifarious and abundant, and not a man alive knows
how to navigate his way through them all. The whereabouts
of all the enemy has laid for the righteous is only in the
omniscient mind of God. If we seek His guidance, the Holy
Spirit will gladly guide our feet past every one of them. But
we must be of upright heart. Indeed, the steps of a good
man—the man or woman of integrity—are ordered by the
Lord (Psalm 37:23).

4. Integrity promises the perpetuation of a godly line,
    blessed and established for many generations.

*Now if you walk before Me as your father David
walked, in integrity of heart and in
uprightness...then I will establish...forever.*

1 Kings 9:4-5

David's integrity before God started something the Lord intended to last forever. Only when David's descendants departed from the right way, did this destiny of blessing get derailed.

The heart of integrity is one that is fully given to God. It is one that takes Him at His Word—concerning all things—and acts accordingly. The man of integrity may falter occasionally along the way, but he gets right back in the race (as David did), looking for mercy and restoration with a grateful heart. He recognizes his absolute dependency on God, clinging unshakably to the Searcher of Hearts. Oh, how it must sadden Father's heart that so few people desire life at this level! So much has been offered to so many, and yet so few take it for His glory.

5.   Integrity catches the ear of the Father.

The sacrifice of the wicked is an abomination to the Lord, but the prayer of the upright is His delight.
Proverbs 15:8

Not only does God hear the prayer of the upright, but He *delights* to hear that prayer. It is so much His pleasure to hear and respond to the fellowship we offer Him in prayer, that He waits for us.

Therefore the Lord will wait that He may be gracious to you.
Isaiah 30:18

The Hebrew word translated *wait* literally means, "to wait earnestly." The Lord does not have a ho-hum attitude toward our times of fellowship with Him, but has deep feelings and serous intentions. Our prayer time is His

115

delight, and should never be entered into lightly. God is inviting us to come into His war room and discuss with Him important matters that will impact whole families and nations for better or for worse. When we have a take-it-or-leave-it attitude toward our times of prayer, we surely disappoint Him.

Christian soldiers who conduct their lives with a high degree of integrity will find the Lord eagerly awaiting their arrival to the prayer closet. God identifies their perfect hearts (not perfect lives), and appreciates that they come to Him with higher levels of faith and devotion than most do. For these, He is ready to pour out His bountiful, gracious blessing.

6. Integrity garners illumination in times of darkness.

Unto the upright there arises light in the darkness.
Psalm 112:4

Have you ever been surrounded by the darkness of a severe trial, and wondered which way to go or which way to turn? Such distressful moments happen in everyone's life, and at these crisis points, many destinies are either shipwrecked forever, or sealed and set for great fulfillment. I have learned that a life of integrity really does matter when these hard times occur. In darkness, we need Heaven's illumination. In times of fear, we need God's courage. In times of outward tossing, we need the inner stability only the Holy Spirit can give us. Integrity will win these special blessings for us, because God bends over backwards to bring illumination to the upright.

7. Integrity garners God's keeping power.

As for me, You uphold me in my integrity, and set me before Your face forever.

Psalm 41:12

God's covenant with Christians provides a remarkable keeping power, an astounding staying power, a rock-solid longevity. But unless we have integrity and an upright heart, this power will be short-circuited.

The forces arrayed against the human family are vicious and many, and regardless of who you are or where you come from, the winds and the rains of life will at times beat against you. A life of integrity will help keep one in good standing with the God who longs to be our strong support in times of trouble.

ENDNOTE

*   Cal Thomas, *The Death of Ethics in America,* Word Publishing, Dallas, London, Sydney, Singapore, 1988, p.13.

10
The Thin Red Line

In English military antiquity, the Thin Red Line described a tested company of soldiers who were positioned on the front lines of the Crown's most crucial battles. Often faced with overwhelming odds, the Thin Red Line was all that stood between a bitter enemy and their comrades in the rear. Each Red Line warrior knew that if their ranks were broken, it would not go well for their army. The enemy would surely pour through the breach like a flood at the breaking of a dam and slaughter their companions. This would be a tragedy worse than death. Therefore the Thin Red Line possessed a hold or die mentality.

The color "red" denoted the cardinal hue of the uniforms worn by these illustrious soldiers. Indeed, when an enemy soldier peered across the aching void called *no man's land*, and beheld these warriors decked in their bright red mantles, a certain dread filled his heart. He knew he was about to tangle with the most lethal warriors of his day—England's elite.

Revival warriors are like that. They are God's Thin Red Line of heroes. They have decided that by life or death they will magnify Christ and advance His Kingdom. They are God's Thin Red Line because they are washed in the crimson blood of their Redeemer. As Heaven's best, they are bulwarks against the insidious schemes and advancements of the evil kingdom. They are the standard the Lord raises against demon powers that come to decimate what is precious to God's heart. In every generation they appear on the human stage to wring decisive victories from situations that appear bleak and hopeless.

They are wilderness-trained shepherds who advance toward demonic giants with nothing but slings and stones, fearlessly destroying that which would defy the living God. (See 1 Samuel 17:10, 26, 45-50.) They are humble private worshippers of the living God, wielding tested weapons forged in the fires of their past. "Heroes are created by popular demand," one man said, "sometimes out of the scantiest materials." Such was David as he faced down the belligerent giant of Gath.

Revival warriors, like Eleazar and Shammah, are champions who stand amidst fields of lentils and barley, defending them against Philistine theft or destruction. Like these heroes of old, Thin Red Liners stand formidably against demonic invasions designed to wrest blessings from the people of God. (See 1 Chronicles 11:12-14; 2 Samuel 23:11-12.)

Thin Red Liners are the heroic wall warriors of Ezekiel 22:30. Searched for but not always found, they answer God's call to build the ramparts through prayer and fasting, that the land not be destroyed.

They are the faithful laborers of Matthew 9:38, crying in days of harvest, "Here am I, Lord, send me!" And as we've mentioned, they are like the warriors of Zebulun and Naphtali in Deborah's day, who risked their lives "on the heights of the battlefield" (Judges 5:18). The mission field is a battlefield.

The Thin Red Line are also the sighing, crying saints of Ezekiel 9:4, who weep over the abominations that turn away God's face from His people. They have the Heaven-mark in their foreheads, distinguishing them as those not to be harmed by the torturous oppressions of end time demons. (See also Revelation 7:3; 9:4.)

They are the Christian disciples who have pledged their hearts and their heads to Heaven, and so will not wilt before the brutality and disdain of malevolent demons and kingdoms of men. (See Revelation 12:11; 2:10.)

The Thin Red Line is comprised of devout men and women who, like the valiant warriors of Jabesh-Gilead, rise up and go all night to recover fallen comrades—those whom Satan displays as trophies in his temples. (See 1 Samuel 31:8-13.)

When a backslider lounges in Satan's temples (wherever the world gathers to sin), the demonic hordes point out and jeer him, claiming the deserter as a trophy of war. But valiant men rise up and go all night (in prayer, fasting and merciful confrontation), and "convert the sinner from the error of his way, save his soul from death, and hide a multitude of sins." (See James 5:19-20.)

No Chocolate Soldiers

According to the great English missionary, C.T. Studd, most believers are like chocolate soldiers, "dissolving in water and melting at the smell of fire." But the Thin Red Line isn't like that. It thrives on combat. Studd wrote:

In peace, true soldiers are captive lions, fretting in their cages. War gives them liberty and sends them, like boys bounding out of school, to obtain their heart's desire or perish in the attempt. Battle is the soldier's vital breath! Peace turns him into a stooping asthmatic. War makes him a whole man again, and gives him the heart, strength, and vigor of a hero.[*]

The most frustrated, grumpy Christians I ever met were people who were called to much higher levels of activity than what they were presently giving themselves to. Some people are natural-born fighters, and if they do not have demons to fight, they'll inevitably turn their guns on their brothers and sisters, and this is dreadful substitute for true war.

In the realm of natural warfare, there are men who call themselves soldiers of fortune. They are mercenaries who so enjoy the thrill of combat that they hire themselves out to nations at war, which need additional forces. War is in their life's blood, and they usually make lousy civilians in times of quiet and peace.

Rapid and Ready Deployment

God's Thin Red Line is deployed for both offensive and defensive warfare. While advancing, they are never bewildered; when entrenched, they are impenetrable. They do not need to wait for the spiritual airwaves over a region to be cleansed of evil despotisms before striking out in evangelistic ferocity. If that was always God's way, then Paul would not have responded so promptly to the Macedonian call (Acts 16:9-10), but would have waited until his prayer warriors had purged the atmosphere above Macedonia of every evil prince before going in. No, beloved, God's warriors advance in the presence of despots and tyrants, be they men or demons, and the hearts of spiritual princes tremble when the Thin Red Line appears on the horizon.

We have friends who recently deployed to a Muslim country in spite of the fact that many in that part of the world hate Christian Americans. Since establishing a beachhead in that country, our friends have seen many

Muslims convert to Christianity. They didn't let the threats from radical Muslims prevent them from going into harm's way to win the lost. In my mind, their determination to make Christ known "by life or by death," has identified our friends as members of God's Thin Red Line.

Bad to the Bone

Revival warriors are bad to the bone. They can fight alongside a large mass of believers, or they can damage Satan's kingdom when operating in small groups or on their own. They can march in rank, or be the stealth fighters who slip quietly behind enemy lines and cut (as it were) the spiritual throats of demonic entities. The Word in their hands is lethal.

> *For the Word of God is living and powerful, and sharper than any two-edged sword... And there is no creature [demon or otherwise] hidden from His sight, but all things are naked and opened to the eyes of Him to whom we must give account.*
>
> Hebrews 4:12-13

The Greek word *trachelizo* in this verse, translated "opened" literally means "to seize and twist the neck." When a warrior forces an adversary into such a vulnerable position, he can do what he wants to him. This is precisely what demons want to do to you, so why not first do it to them?

When Joshua subdued the enemies who resisted his possession of the Promised Land, he ordered his captains to put their feet on the necks of the five pagan kings who had challenged them. This symbolized their absolute subjection to Israel in warfare. (See Joshua 10:24.) The verse in Hebrews reveals that the living, powerful Word of God cannot only expose the attitudes and motives of mankind, but it can also force His spiritual enemies into complete subjection.

Another form of the word *trachelizo* is the word *tracheia*, from which we get the modern term "trachea," or windpipe. Think of what this implies. As a modern day Joshua, each kingdom commando must offer no mercy to the demons thrown down before them. Taking the sharp two-edged sword of the Spirit (Ephesians 6:17), they should decapitate them so they are unable to raise an immediate threat to the welfare of the victims they tormented for so long. Does this signify a literal decapitation? Of course not. But it does denote putting a demon out of commission for an indefinite period of time by binding (or tying him) with a decree moored firmly to God's Word. (See Matthew 12:29; 16:19; Mark 11:23; Job 22:28.) Ponder the importance of the neck to any living creature. Through it run the physiological necessities of life: essential arteries and veins, the throat, the windpipe and larynx, as well as the spinal cord with its complicated system of nerves. What awesome implications are included in the idea of the Word of God exposing the necks of our enemies! What possibilities are ours in this warfare against the forces of darkness! An enemy's exposed neck presupposes his subjugation, and should always precede his elimination.

You have also given me the necks of my enemies, so that I destroyed those who hated me.
                                        Psalm 18:40

I would like to end this chapter with a poem I wrote about The Thin Red Line and its importance to God's work on earth today. I hope it encourages you to move to the front.

God's Thin Red Line

Cold darkness hangs in sky above,
The Thin Red Line appears;
Across the ancient aching void,
The demons brace in fear.
A host of mighty blood-washed saints
Muster in the Light,
With Christ Redeemer's joyous song
Supplying all their might.

As day breaks 'cross the killing fields
Where imps and devils crawl,
A deadness cloaks the souls of men
And binds them to the fall.
A new day dawns on bright red hues
Of mantles soaked in blood,
The blood of Christ on mighty men,
The army that He loves.

Sounds of the trumpet pierce the sky
Where death has ruled the night,
Blasts loud and strong release the throng
And sends it to the fight.
Advancing on the world at large,
God's valiant warriors come;
Till all the world will hear of Christ,
The Son of God's dear love.

With prayer, decree, and mighty song,
They move the kingdom forth;
They preach as men from other worlds,
With power and godly force.

And when the closing effort's made
And final souls are won,
They'll cast their crowns before His feet,
Before the glorious Son.

— M. H.

ENDNOTES

*   C.T. Studd, *The Chocolate Soldier,* World Evangelism for Christ, Int'l., Fort Washington, PA., p. 3.

11
Two Exceptional Armies

By examining the armies of two of Israel's most successful kings, one uncovers many exciting qualities that, if found today in God's spiritual army, will produce many glorious victories as it seeks to liberate humanity from the cruel hand of Satan. These two kings fielded armies that were the terror of the nations around them. The commander of an opposing force would stare out across the aching void with fear and trepidation when the warriors of these two kings appeared on the distant horizon.

Uzziah's Extraordinary Men

Uzziah was a king of Judah who had an illustrious beginning. Because he did what was right in the sight of the Lord in his early years, God favored him with an invincible army. Perhaps we can learn something that will aid us as we face epic battles in the end times.

Moreover, Uzziah had an army ready for battle, which entered into battle by divisions, according to the number of their muster. They were an elite army...and could wage war in great power, to help the king against the enemy. Hence his name spread far, for he was marvelously helped until he was strong.

2 Chronicles 26:11,13,15, NAS

King Uzziah's army was distinguished because it remained fit and *ready for battle.* While the soldiers of surrounding kingdoms grew lazy through frivolous preoccupations, Uzziah's fighting force remained disciplined and brilliantly postured for battle at a moment's notice; instant in season and out of season.

Uzziah's army also entered battle *by divisions.* The entire mass of warriors was divided into various divisions, and yet the men maintained a sense of unity—of connectedness—to the entire body, as well as to their head, King Uzziah.

Each local church or ministry should see itself as a division of spiritual fighters who are connected to something much larger than itself. As a division, it may carry its own colors, wave its own banners, rally to its own battle hymns, etc., but it should never see itself as independent of the Body of Christ in its city, nation, or the rest of the world. Churches that become exclusive and separate from the Christian community in their respective areas, tell themselves that they are the only ones God smiles upon. In reality they become the greatest hindrance to genuine unity in their region. The telltale signs of such deception are seen in a group's criticism and judgment of other churches, as well as in the repulsive and self-important focus they place on their own activities as the only ones that are worth anything. Churches like these actually give power to principalities of division in a region, and their own spiritual pride and arrogance delay great outpourings for years to come. While we may enter battle by divisions, this does not mean that we can be divisive. Neither does it mean that we can separate from the rest of the army and consider ourselves to be the only valid expression of Christ's body in our region. We are members of a worldwide spiritual army. If we think the division of soldiers who occupy another building in our town or city are not doing things right, then we must pray and believe for the Lord to correct what is wrong. May we never put our mouths against them.

Uzziah's army also entered battle *according to the number of their muster.* Not one division of warriors was expected to do more than it was commissioned and equipped to do by its king. In other words, a division of three thousand soldiers was not required to achieve the same results as a division of ten thousand soldiers. Every group had a job to do, every unit had value.

In the Church, the eye is not to say to the ear, "Because you are not an eye, you are worthless!" On the contrary, the eye should thank God for the ear, appreciating that together they help the whole body to function better.

King Uzziah's army was also *an elite* group of fighters. Each member was highly trained and equipped to wage war more effectively than the soldiers of the average army of that period. Uzziah's army was a cut above the rest—a breed apart! Superior training, better discipline, and higher standards by which to be measured, contributed to their greater effectiveness.

Uzziah's army also waged war in *great power,* not ordinary power. Because the Lord was with them, they were terrible in their onset and supernatural in their accomplishments. Unfettered by mere natural abilities, Uzziah's army could move in the power of God's might to win countless victories for its king.

The Church of Jesus is not limited by its own resources either. In our weakness, Christ makes us strong. Because we are inadequate, He becomes our adequacy. Because we lack wisdom, He freely provides His own insight and discretion. As long as the branches abide in the Vine, they will bear much fruit. As long as His army depends solely on Him for its every provision, it will score one victory after another, right up until the time when Jesus returns.

It is also written that Uzziah's army *marvelously helped* him toward the fulfillment of his destiny. As a result, this king's name spread far and wide. He was empowered more than the kings of all other nations.

So what does all this say to you and me? It tells us that, like Uzziah's natural army, the army of Jesus Christ on earth should be a spiritual force of elite warriors second to none in conduct and accomplishment. It should be a highly trained and disciplined host, thoroughly equipped and made ready to consummate the war of the ages in splendid power so that Jesus' name be known and revered far and wide! Subduing kingdoms by faith, putting to flight the armies of aliens, stopping the mouths of demonic lions, and quenching the fires of satanic oppression (Hebrews 11:33-34), Jesus' elite fighters should exercise spiritual dominion until the King Himself returns, and the kingdoms of this world become the kingdom of our God and of His Christ! No believer should expect to do more than what God has enabled him to do, but neither should he plan on doing less than what he is capable of doing in the power of the Holy Ghost.

Unfortunately, our final glimpse of Uzziah's life is one of pride, transgression and destruction (26:16-21). Because of these three sins He was forcefully removed from leadership by both the Lord and his own people. Fortunately, his son, Jotham, reigned in his place, and because he prepared his ways before the Lord, he became mighty, his army remained healthy, and for at least sixteen more years, Israel enjoyed the blessing of God.

A Look at David's Heroes

The Bible records how King David's illustrious command fielded an elite group of special warriors. Strengthening themselves in his kingdom, these fighters became men of renown—revered by one and all. (See 1 Chronicles 11 and 12, and 2 Samuel 23.)

Adino was one impressive fighter who lifted up his spear to slay 800 men at once. Certainly this feat was not accomplished by natural might or power, but by the Spirit of the Lord working in and through him.

Another brilliant warrior was Eleazar. This champion, whose name means "God has helped," stood amidst a field of barley and defied a host of Philistine invaders (even after his companions had fled), and fought them until his hand grew weary. A power not his own then caused his hand to cleave to his sword, and the Lord wrought an outstanding victory on that fateful day. Indeed, when we are weak in our own power, then we are strong with His! By simply refusing to budge from ground his king deemed valuable, Eleazar baffled the desire of an evil host of men and eliminated them in the power of the Spirit. The barley field he defended represents the rich blessings of the Lord that Satan's host desires to steal from God's children. Someone must rise up to fight for those who cannot or will not fight for themselves. Today's commandos must do nothing less than this if victory will be realized.

Eleazar's story causes me to admire the pastors I've known who refused to yield precious spiritual ground to the liberal, anti-Christian forces that sought to hijack and ruin their denominations and the marvelous works begun by godly forefathers and mothers. As modern day heroes, they defy the special-interest factions of their respective organizations, faithfully upholding the Word of God in spite

131

of the heat and scorn incessantly hurled their way.

Another thing I like about Eleazar is his generous attitude toward the men who deserted him at the outset of battle. Rather than despise them when they returned to the battlefield to share in the spoils, he welcomed them. He was unlike many Christians I've known who developed some sort of "woe-is-me" suffering servant complex when they had to do some things by themselves.

Another of David's mighty warriors was Shammah. This man of valor, like Eleazar, stood like a stone wall during a Philistine attack when all of his men had deserted him. This solitary scrapper positioned himself in the midst of a field of lentils and defended it, slaying an entire troop of enemy warriors as the battle intensified. Through him the Lord wrought another spectacular victory!

Abishai was another mighty man who made a name for himself in warfare. This devoted warrior lifted up his spear against 300 enemy fighters and served them a crushing defeat in the heat of the day. But that's not all! Wherever and whenever valor was called for, Abishai distinguished himself as a man of great worth. (See 1 Samuel 26:6-9; 2 Samuel 3:30; 16:9; 21:15-17; 1 Chronicles 18:12-13.)

As a pastor, I've been blessed with an Abishai or two through the years. These have been men and women who were quick to defend my name and honor when both were attacked. They didn't see me as a flawless leader, but they saw me as a God-called leader destined to touch many lives with the gospel. They knew they were called to uphold and assist me through the difficult times as well as the good.

Beloved, determine that you will be an Abishai to your spiritual leaders. Don't serve and defend them only because they do everything right (David certainly had his failures), but because you are called to serve and honor them for God's glory. They are His servants, ordained to fulfill a certain, valuable destiny. Help them to do it, and you'll be rewarded richly at the Judgment Seat of Christ.

Benaiah was another of David's impressive warriors. A man great of deeds, Benaiah single-handedly slew two lion-like champions of Moab. He also went down into a pit and slew a lion on a snowy day, depicting the readiness of a commando to fight in all weathers and in all locations. In addition to these mighty acts, Benaiah slew an impressive man of the Egyptians—with the man's own spear! Anointed commandos take what Satan means for harm, turn it around, and use it for God's glory.

David had other dynamic warriors as well. Three unique men stood nearby when he was in the cave of Adullam. These attentive warriors stood close enough to hear their king's quiet longing for water from the well at Bethlehem's gate. David's wish became their command! Without thought for their own lives, the three sprang into action, broke through the Philistine lines, and fetched the water their king desired. So touched by the devotion of these three men, David could only take the water they brought him and pour it on the ground as an offering to God.

All of the mighty warriors in David's army were normal men until times got tough. They then were transformed by the power of the Holy Spirit into the awesome fighters we read about! In spiritual warfare we can have similar results if we will commit as deeply to Jesus as they did to David.

David's Mighty Men

Centuries ago when David was king,
An elite group of warriors arose.
They were strong from the start
And loyal of heart;
In battle, they kept on their toes.

With ruthless resolve they fought for their king,
With whatever they had in their hands;
With blood, sweat, and tears,
Over several long years,
They emerged as his men of renown.

Adino was there, endued with God's grace,
A man not of brawn nor great power;
But anointed with love,
And strength from above,
He defeated eight hundred one hour.

At Pasdammim's ground, David's enemies found,
A field full of barley they wanted.
But as they'd soon learn,
Eleazar stood firm,
And the Philistine's wishes were thwarted!

Despite their bold aim, Eleazar did claim,
That ground for his king's unfurled banner.
With hand froze to sword,
He vanquished this horde -
They fell before his holy anger!

Shammah by name, was another great man,
For David his value was high;
Resplendent with class,
And Holy Ghost sass,
He slaughtered his foes hip and thigh!

There were many great days, in Abishai's blaze,
When the king was defended with honor;
Equipped with great zeal –
The kind that is real -
Of combat there wasn't one fonder.

To fight with a spear, this boy didn't care,
Whether Saul or a Philistine giant;
Anointed with fire,
And Holy Ghost ire,
To enemies he was defiant!

Now let's not forget Benaiah the great,
The son of a man from Kabzeel,
Warm weather or not,
This warrior was hot,
For battle he had a great zeal.

When Moab's choice heroes confronted him strong,
Like lions aroused from their bed,
Benaiah got ruthless
And saw them as toothless,
And struck them until they were dead!

Remember the day when raw winds were blowing,
And cold snow had covered the land?
Into a pit
Benaiah did slip,
And slaughtered a lion by hand.

Time ne'er can tell of the giant Egyptian,
A champion five cubits tall;
Confronting this beast,
Benaiah believed,
"The taller the harder they fall!"

With righteous bold anger, and no time to spare,
He wrestled the spear from his hand,
And as with the lion,
The day it was dying,
He took down and slaughtered the man.

What more can be said of these valiant young men,
Who served in their time with devotion?
Except that today,
We can serve the same way
The Redeemer by whom we are chosen.

Our fight's not with flesh, but with spirits unseen,
With demons' high evil strong bastions,
But with Jesus our Lord
And with Holy Ghost sword,
The outcome is never in question.

— M. H.

David's Regular Army

Not only was David's army graced with valiant
individuals like the ones we just examined, but great
numbers of men from the tribes of Israel gathered to his
side to comprise the regular army. According to 1 Chronicles
12, these soldiers were skilled with all weapons of war;
were lethal with both the left and right hands when hurling

136

stones and shooting arrows; were efficient in handling shield and buckler; had the deeply-focused and fearsome faces of lions; and were as swift and agile as gazelles in the mountains. A mighty unction for battle crowned David's army, and today when a man's ways please the Lord, a similar unction for war results.

Combat Arms or Arms Support?

Every successful army divides its people into two main groups: Those who face the enemy on the front lines of battle, and those who "stay by the supplies" (1 Samuel 25:13). Not only do the arms support people stay at home by the supplies, but they also manage all the nitty-gritty details the combat arms people cannot handle while they are out on the front. According to the Bible, we need both groups in the Church, and one group is no more important than the other. In fact, when David's fighters tried to establish a difference of importance between the two groups, he rebuked them, establishing a statute and ordinance to prevent it from happening again. (See 1 Samuel 30:22-25.)

Praise God for all who comprise the mighty army of Yeshua! The combined number of all He has in Heaven and on earth is staggering and incalculable. One day in the future, the Lord Jesus will assemble all of us together in one place, and we will be rendered speechless when we see how many of us there really are. On that day, saints from Heaven and earth will be drawn together by the millions to see a splendid mounted Rider descending from Heaven on a glorious white steed to take up His throne, Jerusalem! And all the tribes and families of the earth will either mourn because of Him, or be blessed beyond comprehension by His magnificent unstoppable arrival.*

ENDNOTE

* The following list of Scriptures reveal the awesomeness of Christ's return to earth. Many people will embrace His coming, while the majority will be terrified by it.

1 Thessalonians 4:16-17; 2 Thessalonians 2:8; Jude 14; Revelation 1:7; Zechariah 12:9-10; Revelation 19:11-16; Psalm 22:27-28; Revelation 1:7; 6:12-17.

12
Cut Down to Size

"The Lord is with you, you mighty man of valor!" Such were the first words Gideon heard from the Angel of the Lord as he threshed wheat in a concealed winepress (Judges 6:11-12). In Israel, everything was out of place. The people who rightfully owned the land were hiding like varmints. The people who did not own the land were running around acting, as we say around here, like tall hog at the trough. I am sure the young man's first reaction to the Angel's startling words was comical. He probably looked quickly about to see who the angel was speaking to. He certainly didn't see himself as a mighty man of valor, and he couldn't see that the Lord was with him.

When Gideon realized the Angel was addressing him, he responded almost in curt tones: "If the miracle working God of our father's is with us, then why has He allowed us to get in such dire straights? Gosh!" Gideon protested, "The Midianites torment us to the point that we're all afraid to come out of our hiding places! We're like foxes hiding in the dens and caves of the hills!"

But God didn't see Gideon just the way Gideon saw himself. Jehovah Sabaoth never sees one who is a warrior by blood in such a confining, earthbound way. He always views us from Heaven's lofty heights, and through the cloudless vision of eternity.

Once the Angel of the Lord revealed Gideon's true identity, he sent him out to gather an army with which to defeat the enemy. When the process of gathering and fielding this army was accomplished, Gideon commanded his own Thin Red Line of heroes. They were 300 proven warriors, ready for battle.

However, before Gideon was ready for battle, a paring down process had to occur. So God instructed him to send away all the fearful soldiers. Their timid hearts rendered them unfit for the coming fight. Such a fear is highly contagious, and can negatively affect the attitude of other soldiers. In an earlier generation, Moses had also dismissed fearful warriors, lest their frightened hearts extinguish the battle-fire in the hearts of their comrades. (See Deuteronomy 20:8.) Nothing saps a victory consciousness from the heart of a warrior like the enemy we know as Fear. Where Faith moves one forward in life, Fear pushes him backwards. Where Faith gratifies and calls God's righteous power into action, fear pleases Satan and calls his wicked power into action. Each human soul has the authority to choose which it will be. Every man or woman has the authority to call one or the other forces into action concerning their own life.

Once the fearful had departed from Gideon, ten thousand men remained—ready to go into battle. But were they really ready? Obviously not, because God instructed Gideon to submit them to a simple but revealing test in order to determine who the elite really were. As the remaining soldiers went to drink from the water flowing from the Well of Harod, Gideon observed how each man got his drink. Whoever laid down his weapon, and got down on his hands and knees to drink was considered careless, and therefore unfit for the coming battle. However, whoever simply dropped to his knees, holding fast to his weapon with the one hand, while bringing water to his mouth with the other, was deemed ready to go up against the enemy. This method of drinking revealed a clear-headedness and vigilance that passed God's inspection. As a result of this simple test only 300 warriors remained to become the warriors who would wreak havoc in the enemy camp.

As the leader of spiritual warriors, I often watch the behavior of the folks who say they want to follow me into an arena of warfare. Be it intercessory prayer, evangelistic work, or some other aggressive form of activity carried on for the purpose of depopulating hell and populating Heaven, I observe the way the people involve themselves. If they exhibit a nonchalant, take-it-or-leave-it attitude in their approach to ministry, I realize that they lack what's necessary to keep them on the front lines. In time they will either become casualties, or simply drift away. The Word tells us to remain sober and vigilant, "because your adversary the devil walks about like a roaring lion, seeking whom he may devour" (1 Peter 5:8). The non-vigilant eventually get devoured.

Opposing Gideon and his 300 were Midianites and Amalekites who were "as numerous as locusts" (Judges 7:12). It appeared as though it would be a lop-sided battle; but when God is on your side it's always lop-sided in the opposite direction than one would expect. Wasn't it Jonathan who said, "for nothing restrains the Lord from saving by many or by few," just moments before he slaughtered a superior Philistine force with no one but his armor-bearer beside him? (See I Samuel 14:1-13.) The size of an opponent's army doesn't intimidate the Lord at all; neither should it intimidate us. In fact, the Lord enjoys claiming victory in fights where only a few of His warriors are involved. In this way, no one can claim success based on the size and strength of his own resources. (See Judges 7:2.)

Beloved, Christian warriors at the end of this age should have the same humble understanding that Jonathan and Gideon had. Placing their faith in God, they do not base the likelihood of their success on the natural abilities they possess. Neither do they base the likelihood of their failure on the number of adversaries arrayed against them. Both the onset and outcome of battle must be based on what God has said, as well as on what He has told them to do. So rarely do numbers have anything to do with God's word to us, that we need to dismiss them altogether unless God brings it up. Let us never judge the length of our sword by the size of our people! When David did this, a plague decimated the people from Dan to Beersheba to the sum of seventy thousand men (1 Chronicles 21:1-14). Rather than assess our military might, let us assess the Lord's might, relying on His power alone to put us over in combat. According to the Lord's calculations, one can put a thousand to flight, and two can put ten thousand to flight when the battle is the Lord's. Indeed, pound for pound, some of the most powerful outreaches in the world are small in number. Their ministries are far-reaching and powerfully effective because they are moving on a word from their Commander-in-Chief, and not on a confidence in their own natural resources. Mark Twain was correct when he said, "It's not the size of the dog in the fight that matters, but the size of the fight in the dog!" Beloved, when God provides the fight inside of us, we are invincible!

The Lord is Watching You

Few Christians realize that the Lord's eyes are not simply looking to show Himself strong in their behalf, but they are also looking to see who He *cannot* trust and bless with His power and anointing. As Gideon's warriors approached

142

warfare in two different ways, with two different attitudes, so God's people tend to do the same today. For this reason, the Lord listens to the words we say, just as much as He watches the behavior we exhibit. The power volume on our words, and the anointing level in our bodies are to a large part determined by what God hears and sees happening in our day-to-day lives.

A verse in John' gospel says a lot about why Jesus' ministry was so effective and powerful:

For the one whom God has sent speaks the words of God, for God gives the Spirit without limit.
John 3:34, NIV

This one verse speaks volumes to those of us who would be used by God in these days. Because the Father could totally trust Jesus to speak His Word, and only things that were in accordance with His Word, He was able to anoint Him with power in an unlimited measure. The same Holy Spirit Jesus had is available to you and me today, and we should be doing the "greater works" He told us about (John 14:12). But all-too-often we short-circuit God's power by our faithless words and conduct, and send His eyes searching for someone else. Beloved, if we would only allow the Holy Spirit to do a quick work taming our tongues and purifying our conduct, we could get on with being the mighty vessels of His glory that He intended all along!

13
Seeing From God's Perspective

Having God's perspective is crucial to the well rounded and effective Christian. Without it, one loses balance, perception, and courage. I often say that if the believer can maintain God's viewpoint, he will keep his mind, and if he can keep his mind, he will keep the high ground.

Numbers 13 relates how twelve spies went into the Promised Land to gather information valuable to Israel's upcoming conquests. Ten of the twelve returned from the reconnaissance mission terrified by giants they saw and deemed too big and fearsome to defeat. They said that they were mere grasshoppers before these formidable sons of Anak.

> *And there we saw the giants...and we were in our own sight as grasshoppers, **and so we were in their sight.***
>
> Numbers 13:33

This statement is revealing! It tells us that if we view ourselves as grasshoppers before our enemies, then that is precisely how they will see us. However, if we can see ourselves through God's eyes, as being more than conquerors through Jesus Christ, and well able to take the land for His kingdom, then our enemies will tremble when we approach. Like horses and dogs, demons can recognize

145

and exploit fear within a human being. But they also recognize and respect faith and godly confidence. Fear within us incites a defiant challenge, but strong confidence backs it down. Therefore we must develop a giant-killer mentality for the days ahead. We must allow the Holy Spirit to place His confidence inside of us by deliberately and systematically filling our hearts with God's Word. The Lord means to bring the Church into an awesome inheritance in the coming seasons of harvest, but we must have the mind of Christ concerning who we are in Him *if* we will receive it.

Seize God's Provision

Beloved, avoid a careless attitude when it comes to developing your spiritual viewpoint and claiming your inheritance in Christ. Grow up into Him in all things, and aggressively possess your possessions!

> *[God] is wooing you from the jaws of distress, to a spacious place free from restriction, to the comfort of your table laden with choice food.*
>
> Job 36:16, NIV

From this verse we can see that the Lord has prepared a table for us, and loaded it with benefits. But it is also obvious that this table is situated in the presence of our enemies (Psalm 23:5). Not to worry though, because the Lord has afforded His people the faith and patience necessary to fight through all satanic resistance and set a chair at the table. Possibly this is what Jesus was talking about when He said, "Indeed, from the days of John the Baptizer until this moment, the kingdom of heaven is being taken by storm, and the strong and forceful ones claim it for themselves eagerly" (Matthew 11:12, Wuest Expanded Translation).

In His kindness, God has spread before us a table laden with all manner of spiritual and physical blessings, and Jesus bids us come. On that table are generous helpings of power over sin, healing for the body, and freedom from mental torment. In Matthew 15:26, Jesus says that healing and deliverance are "the children's bread," spread bountifully on the covenant table of God. But between us and that table are obstacles that must be hurdled or removed by the violent resolve of each Christian. The giants of sin, sickness, poverty, laziness, disobedience and fear are the sons of Anak (the giants) through which we must force ourselves if we will enjoy heaping platefuls of God's blessings. We must learn to fight for what's ours! He is a sorry soldier indeed who believes he can overcome without fighting and claim a crown without conflict. The victor's crown, *stephanos,* is only awarded to those who endure the temptation to yield to hardship and quit. (See James 1:12.)

There was a day in my life when a physical giant named rheumatoid arthritis rose up against me. This debilitating disease worked overtime for a period of four years as it twisted and swelled various joints in my body. Because I was ignorant of certain undying truths related to the cross of Christ, I figured I was destined to suffer the horrors of the arthritic to my dying day.

The teaching I had received up to that point in my life did very little to prepare me for such an imposing giant, and because I saw myself as helpless before it, I simply laid down and allowed it to dominate me.

However, my story didn't end there. In 1975, one year after I was saved, God's truth burst into my life, and I began to learn that Jesus not only bore my sin on the cross, but He bore my sickness and disease as well. Jesus' blood officially redeemed me from the curse of arthritis. By comparing such verses as Galatians 3:13 with Deuteronomy 28:22, I saw that arthritis was definitely a curse from which I was redeemed. As I continued to meditate on this eternal truth, and as I made it a part of my daily confession, I began to experience release from the arthritis and its awful effects. The victory wasn't realized immediately, but with a growing knowledge of the Word of God concerning my redemption, and with ever-increasing amounts of faith and patience being established in my heart, I was well on my way to freedom; I was pressing through to the table.

Today I live in victory over this dreaded disease. I am grateful because God revealed His truth to me, and I am healed because I received that truth, allowing it to become life and medicine to my flesh and bones (Proverbs 4:20-22). No longer do I see myself as a helpless grasshopper before my enemies, but as a giant killer, I am determined to experience God's power for myself, as well as to help secure it for those who yet sit in bondage to the giants of sin, sickness and spiritual death. Will you join me?

It is Time to Advance!

If we are reading the signs of the times accurately, and if our interpretations of the prophetic Scriptures are correct, the strong-armed powers of many anti-Christian nations will soon be shaken to the teeth. Their iron grip on the masses will be loosened, and the delusions under which their citizens have been forced to live will evaporate in the penetrating rays of the glorious gospel. When these realms are shattered, the doors to countless people groups will open wide to the millions of evangelists who are presently laboring in prayer and limited opportunities. They will go forth in that hour to swing the sickle of the Lord and reap the harvest of the world, gathering it into the Kingdom of

God. In Revelation 14:16, we see that this time of reaping will be tremendously intense, and it will be accomplished in an amazingly short period of time.

Therefore, beloved, it is time for those who have been sleeping to wake up! Do not let this hour pass you by. It is even now upon us. The Scripture says, "He who sleeps in harvest is a son who causes shame" (Proverbs 10:5). No sincere Christian desires to be a source of shame during the harvest hour, but if he sleeps when he should be working, shame will become his bitter cup.

It is thrilling to see what God is doing around the world. While the news media makes it appear like the Devil has everything going his way, the truth is that God is on the move, executing His game plan flawlessly. And we are on His winning team! If there were never any setbacks, it wouldn't be a contest. If there were no casualties, it wouldn't be a war. But regardless of all the enemy is doing to hold off God's purposes, the mighty Kingdom is steadily advancing like a giant D-9 bulldozer, pushing everything before it toward God's desired end.

The masses await a genuine visitation from God, and they will have it! The revival of New Testament Christianity worldwide will be awesome in the days to come. Hundreds of millions will come to know Jesus as their only Potentate and sovereign Lord. Hundreds of oppressed people groups will hear the gospel and respond eagerly. Satan's hold is indeed weakening in response to the worldwide prayer and warfare of the saints.

Many Islamic nations, long opposed to the preaching of the gospel, will soon burst open as Holy Spirit explosions shake their nations in spite of the threats and persecutions of militant Muslims God may even use the armies of sanctioned (not perfect) nations as a terrible swift sword to

149

open up dark regions to the gospel. When Paul spoke of the fullness of the Gentiles coming into the Church in the last days (Romans 11:25), his prophetic eye also saw the millions of people who presently suffer beneath the oppressive paws of Islamic mullahs. The Lord is about to "make bare His holy arm" (Isaiah 52:10) in scores of these gospel-resistant nations, and when He flexes His spiritual muscles, every principality and ruler of darkness will fall back in terror!

The west (North America and Europe) continue to ripen for the gigantic awakening God told us is coming. Although cold orthodoxy and a terribly compromised presentation of the Word of God have taken their toll on the Church in developed countries, God is now birthing a valiant generation of men and women who are repelled by mere form and religion, and who are returning to an authentic style of Christianity not seen since the days of the first apostles. These are people who drink freely from "the river of [God's] pleasures" (Psalm 36:8); they are fire and glory people—a growing host of men and women who want all of God there is to have! Out of this revived and radiant Church there will come a flood of signs and wonders like the world has not seen before, and multitudes will be swept gloriously into the kingdom of God!

Latin America is also reeling beneath a move of God's power that is difficult for the natural mind to comprehend. Although the "isms" (communism and occultism), as well as cold church orthodoxy, claimed supremacy in this region for years, vital Christianity has done nothing but advance in recent years, aggressively challenging every demonic claim to the people who live there. The occurrences of genuine signs and wonders sweeping Central and South America will continue to edge into North America and baffle the minds of the experts, skeptics, and orthodox deadheads. Men who have raised the dead and cleansed the lepers in the heated jungles ringing the Caribbean will advance on America to show ministers how to do more than just preach a good message. Many of America's super conferences will remain closed to these third world commandos, but in time the polished conference superstars seen in the ads of glossy Christian magazines will humbly and gratefully embrace them for what they can teach the North American Church. Satan's religious stranglehold will finally be broken from off the teeming millions who profess a form of godliness, but who deny the power thereof.

China's harvest is perhaps the most awesome on record. Millions of people are being saved behind the Bamboo Curtain by a Church that has learned to thrive in spite of crushing persecution. China, and other nations of the Pacific ring, will soon send forth some of the most powerful world-changers that anyone has ever seen. A veritable army of oriental Christians will invade Asia and the Middle East with a gospel that they have learned to die for. They will be the ones to reach the Islamic and Hindu peoples. This awesome army will precede the natural two hundred million man army that is destined to march to the Battle of Armageddon. I believe they will reap a massive harvest as they traverse earth's most populous region, giving everyone a chance to receive Christ before the kings of the east sweep through, killing what the Bible claims, will be one third of earth's population. (See Revelation 9:14-16; 16:12.)

Africa is presently swaying beneath the weight of one of the greatest awakenings the world has ever witnessed. Even while bad news fills the headlines, millions of Africans are being ushered into God's family. Although an exhausting marathon is being run against the forces of Islam for the souls of Africa's millions, Jesus Christ, the living Lord of glory, is emerging as undisputed victor on this once dark continent! Massive gospel crusades, conducted by world-renowned evangelists, are now counting millions of people in attendance. As far as the eye can see, the crusade grounds are covered with hungry seekers, and multiplied millions are being saved! This glorious phenomenon will continue unabated as the Lord of the harvest wraps up this present age.

But what is even more exciting is the unfettered commitment of the gospel foot soldiers who faithfully penetrate Africa's darkest regions with power evangelism. As these spiritual commandos enter houses and huts, market places and villages, the Lord confirms the Word they preach with signs and outstanding wonders. Every argument proffered by the enemy falls before the raw, manifest power of the mighty God!

The islands of the sea are also feeling the impact of the gospel. Already, spiritual invasion forces have established impressive beachheads in thousands of seaside cities and villages, and the gospel is penetrating every strata of society. The battles being waged on these island nations is indeed intense, but as the smoke clears away after each violent skirmish with the forces of darkness, the kingdom of God emerges in victory!

Some of the most anointed praise and ministry teams the world has ever known are also coming from the islands. Fashioned and polished as anointed arrows, and concealed in obscure quivers, these ministers of power will soon come forth to impact the entire world for God!

Beloved, the times are exciting! No matter where you look, the fields are "already white for harvest!" (John 4:35).

The members of our church who have a heart for souls are enjoying a time of harvest like they never experienced before. It seems like everybody in our region is opened to at least hear the gospel. But we have to go after them. We cannot wait for them to wander into our churches. Therefore, we are infiltrating hospitals, malls, supermarkets and homes, and we are seeing a positive response to the message of Jesus. It hasn't always been that way where we live, but our persistent prayers are paying off.

For many years a faithful remnant has gathered in our church on Monday nights for three hours of praise and intercessory prayer. At times it has been hard, but we are committed to the outcome. Come rain, snow or sleet, there are always people who turn up to pray and show the Lord that we are dead serious about our desire for revival and awakening in this region. The fruit of this commitment is now appearing. He is beginning to show Himself strong on our behalf. He is healing the sick and saving the lost. A genuine brand of unity is beginning to occur among the pastors and churches in our area. He is moving on the hearts of pastors to want a region-wide revival to touch every church. What God is doing in our region, He will gladly do in yours. If you can but rally the troops for spiritual prayer and warfare, roust them from their comfort zones, and send them into the harvest fields, you will witness a positive and powerful result.

A Word to Those Who Feel Left Out

I exhort those of you who labor strictly on a local level to hold fast in faith for things to happen where you are. Just look around you. Those people, who until now have been hardened or indifferent to the gospel, will suddenly acquire an insatiable thirst to know the living God. Do not allow their present reaction to your witness to defeat you. The effect of God's Spirit on the hearts of men and women in these last days is going to be profound. Use your time wisely by preparing, by training hard to become the best you can be, and by being faithful to your spiritual leaders. Your diligence will pay off—just wait and see.

OTHER CHIP HILL BOOKS

FRONT LINE WARFARE: is an instruction book for believers who find themselves in the trenches for God's Kingdom. Many uplifting and practical nuggets of truth designed to help you succeed in life's battles are found within the pages of this end-times manual. 230 pages of straightforward, no-nonsense teaching for the serious disciple of Christ.

$9.00

INVISIBLE WILDERNESS: The Appalachian Mountains in 1755 were a harsh and dangerous wilderness. A pioneer named Andrew Woodlief was called of God to invade the savagery of this wilderness with the gospel of Jesus Christ. It didn't matter that both a natural and a spiritual frontier opposed him; he was determined to accomplish his mission. Against all odds, Andrew battles the ignorance of sin-bound men, as well as the treachery of a well-developed demonic army - and wins! "*Invisible Wilderness*" will show you the gospel as it should be presented - in power and with great resolve. The name of Andrew Woodlief will be etched forever in your heart as an example of devotion and spiritual militancy, when you encounter the unseen forces of darkness that are bound to arise in these days. **$8.00**

MANTLES OF ANOINTING: explores many of the special anointings God has for His people - those divine enablements the Church needs in order to be effective and fruitful in this fallen world. Some of the special anointings covered in this volume are the mantles of healing, spiritual warfare, the scribe and many more. This little book is a best seller, and promises to encourage your effectiveness in the ministry. 63 pages. **$7.00**

DYNAMICS OF REVIVAL: A Christian revival of immense proportions is currently breaking onto the world. Many have not comprehended what is involved in such mighty outpourings of the Spirit, and so they fear, dismiss or fight it outright. The time has come for people everywhere to understand and flow into all God is doing as He manifests His glory amidst those of us "upon whom the ends of the ages has come." *Dynamics* is for those seeking understanding and historical validation of God's present move. It was written to encourage your own personal revival, as well as to stir and renew your mission in this great flood of God's glory. **$10.00**

For details about purchasing any or many of these books, please send a check, made payable to:

"Word of Faith Bookstore"
P. O. Box 276
Monterey, VA 24465

and include $2.50 for Shipping & Handling Charges.

Sorry, but we are not set up to accept credit cards at this time. Any questions, please call (540) 468-2592, or email us at *highrsvt@cfw.com.*

_____NOTES_____

Impac **Chris** **ian** **Books**

332 Leffingwell Ave., Suite 101
Kirkwood, MO 63122

AVAILABLE AT YOUR LOCAL BOOKSTORE, OR YOU MAY
ORDER DIRECTLY. Toll-Free, order-line only M/C, DISC,
or VISA 1-800-451-2708.

Visit our Website at *www. impactchristianbooks.com*

Write for *FREE* Catalog.